Qi

Ql

By

CW00495510

Quiche Separabit

Copyright

Published by Michael Collins

Copyright © Michael Collins 2019

The story's in this book are from my own imagination, all my characters and events in this book are fictitious and any resemblance to real people living or dead are purely coincidental apart from my recipes of course.

*****

For my lovely wife Mandy for her valuable input into my book and putting up with my daft ways

Also, my family, friends and neighbours for testing my food

Special thanks to my army colleague and friend Alex Kurlandzki for the title for my book

2

BOOKS BY THE AUTHOR

ACC TO 4/7TH RDG IN 22 YEARS

TIME WAITS FOR NO MAN

THE LOST DRAGOON 1

GHOST TOWN 2

MIRROR MIRROR 3

FREAKSHOW 4

CRANYAM COVE 5

THE QUIET ROOM 6

THE CRYPT 7

THE HANGMANS CHAIR 8

THE BLUE HAZE 9

ELBER TRENTS CHRISTMAS 10

ESCAPE FROM THE AFTERLIFE 11 (out soon)

QUICHE SEPARABIT

*****

This book is dedicated to all my Regimental friends and colleague's past, present and those no longer with us.

FOREWORD

Thank you very much for buying Quiche Separabit and I sincerely hope you enjoy my catering escapades from my military days plus the recipes I have prepared for this book. I served in the British army for twenty two years fifteen of which were with the ACC (Army Catering Corps) then in 1985 I rebadged to my regiment the 4/7th Royal Dragoon Guards for my final seven years, I am proud to say that this regiment was my first and only posting and my personal biography (ACC to 4/7th RDG in 22 years) is still selling for me on the Amazon kindle. Firstly for my military colleagues no matter who you are or where you served, I am sure that Quiche Separabit will bring back some of the memories of those cold days on Soltau and Hohne in west Germany and secondly for my civilian friends I hope it gives you an insight into the ration packs that we were issued with and the type of food we squaddies ate while on exercise.

As a young lad cooking was never a career option for me it was a spur of the moment thing when I first joined the army back in November 1970. Through the years I have always classed myself as a good all-round cook and I have never aspired to be like some of the top chefs of today if you are looking for cordon bleu cooking then you have got the wrong book. Over the years I have gathered my knowledge of catering from the basics I was taught in training and the people I met and worked with during my army years which results in the type of cooking that I do now and that is simple good food. This is not a cookbook which is trying to prove how good I am, far from it, I am just an average bloke who is retired with plenty of time on my hands who wants to show people how we cooks adapted the military compo rations and turned them into outstanding meals with the aid of a few extras such as flour, baking powder, custard powder, herbs and spices, tinned tomatoes, or anything we could get hold of that we stole from the main camp kitchen before we were deployed into the field. We still got stick from the troops who would often call us slop jockeys, cabbage mechanics, Andy caps commandos, it was just squaddie banter which was part of being a cook and it just went over our shoulders, we would jokingly stick two fingers up and tell them to fuck off.

On a cold military exercise after we had finished work we would sit around the burners like bunched up gnomes with a beer in one hand and a fag in the other, we would chat in true squaddie style, talking about sex and telling dirty jokes, plus what we could do with the compo the next day. Some great inspiration and ideas came from these mini piss ups, quite a few are in this book, some of our compo experiments were disasters which failed to impress us or the troops, but others were outstanding. As cooks in the field we all learned from each other, each of us would contribute our own ideas when it came to compo which we all shared together, I have to say some of my best times were spent in a static field kitchen. I am not perfect by any means and I make mistakes, so yes! I do get it wrong. a few days ago, for example I was experimenting on fish cakes for this book everything had gone okay with the preparation, I took the photos and was ready to go, but when I cooked them, they broke up in the pan I had made a right bollocks of them. Not a problem though I sat down and ate them, I did them again and put extra egg yolks in. I was taught that once you get something wrong you will always remember your mistakes. People ask me for example the weights to make Yorkshire puddings and I say one cup of flour one cup of milk, water, salt and a couple of eggs, they just look at me and ask, 'Don't you weigh it? and I reply, 'No! However, throughout this book I will be giving you a few weights and measures in imperial or metric but be prepared for a bit of this and slack handful of that. Also, I want to stress to you about the oven temperatures, I have given the temperatures that I use and they work for me but just beware that all ovens are different so use your own judgement from the settings I have given.

I decided that to make this book more interesting I would compare my recipes with a lot of the composite rations which we were issued with during my army years 1970 to 1993 plus some of the field equipment we used. I thought that this would not only interest my army colleagues but my civilian friends too and that it would also give an insight into the food that we squaddies consumed on manoeuvres, or in a war zone for that matter. Most of the food in this book is the type of stuff I do for my family and friends and it's all tried and tested. At the top of the page I have put a few photos of the composite rations that you will read a lot about in this book, I would have loved to have found a menu sheet from the old 10 man compo packs from A to G so you could have seen for yourselves what type of grub the troops ate. These meals were loaded with calories between 3500 to over 4000 per man per day for obvious reasons and after a week on this stuff when we had to go, well, I don't think I will explain that and leave it to your imagination. What I will say though is that the compo food was bloody good stuff and very versatile for us cooks. A lot of the story's will be compo related and I will try and explain to the best of my knowledge how we transformed the compo into awesome and imaginative food. Also a couple of my old friends will be making an appearance, Lefty (The cowboy) Wright and the sex mad Seedy Simpson, Seedy was a great cook and friend of mine and he thought he was god's gift to woman, he would shag anything that breathed unaided, he was also a master with compo and he knew every cowboy trick in the book, I learned a lot from him in the time I knew him and he gave me some good tips on compo too.

The idea of writing a cook book scared me because most of you can cook in your own way anyway, some of the recipes in this book are easy and you may have your own versions of them, this book is about my recipes and my versions. It took me a while to plan how I would present Quiche Separabit especially with 450 photographs which kept moving when I put my demo chapter through the kindle previewer, in the end I resolved this by putting them in a collage which solved the problem of the moving photographs. For me to write a cook book with hundreds of recipes was out of the question, even I am not that good and it would probably have taken me forever. I decided to put down my fifty favourite recipes from over the years with my take on them plus a little story of how they came about. Please don't expect Jamie Oliver, Ramsey or Escoffier type recipes in this book, this is about straight forward home cooking for the family, the recipes are simple and easy to follow but with my own professional touch plus there is no messing about with fancy ingredients and of course the photos will guide you. There will be a few weights and measures but they are few and far between, a bit of this and a bit of that is the way forward, let your imaginations do the cooking. I like good, tasty food which is quick to put together and doesn't cost a fortune and looks good. People compliment me on the photos of my food and how good it looks on facebook, I was always taught that if it looks good it tastes good, one of my old chef instructors once told me that you always eat with your eyes first. Prepare for a journey through my army years and you will see how the military composite rations influenced and gave me inspiration to adapt my recipes from the beginning of my catering career to the present day. I hope you enjoy Quiche Separabit as a stand-alone read or recipe book or maybe both. **MC**

Table of Contents

QUICHE

       Let's start with one of my favourites and I can tell you that over the years I have literally made tons of this stuff, it was also one of the first things I made while on manoeuvre's in Germany back in 1971. The compo cheese had a soft rubbery texture similar to Edam and I loved it especially in a sandwich with the compo strawberry jam, however the compo margarine that we put on the bread was a bit dire, but it was okay for cooking and making pastry and maybe using as axle grease on a Bedford. As a young inexperienced cook, I thought going on exercise with these ten-man ration packs would be a doddle, all I would need was a can opener a couple of cooking pots and a wooden spoon, how wrong and amazed I was. In those early days I would learn to roll out the pastry for lining the 20x10x2 baking trays, if I didn't have a rolling pin, I would use an unopened stewed steak tin or an empty coke bottle. Using compo in the field was all about improvisation that was the fun of it, if I didn't have a chopping board, I would use the outer hard cardboard sleeve from the actual compo packs, empty cans were used as pastry cutters, there were a couple of plastic lids in each pack that were used for sealing opened tins and were very handy, using a hammer and a nail we would punch holes in the bottom of empty cans to make flour dusters when rolling pastry, the sugar tins we would empty out then carefully bend the lid back to form an handle and a handy drinking mug hehe.

If I was making quiche in the field, I would open both ends of the cheese can and push the cheese out and dice it as fine as I could unless I had the luxury of a cheese grater it was hard work when you had twenty tins to open. I would then open lots of the dried milk and add it to water then whisk in the issued eggs and the diced compo cheese, a bit of salt and pepper then pour it into the pastry case ready for the oven. If we had onions, we would chop them up and in they would go, at the time I thought this was an amazing achievement especially out in the middle of nowhere. As my experience grew, I started experimenting with chopping the compo luncheon meat or bacon grill into the quiche to make it taste more savoury.

Years ago in a busy barrack kitchen we would make huge trays of this and serve it up for lunch, the recipe at the time was from the MACS (Manuel of army catering) a good book by the way and I still sometimes use it now and again for pastries and puddings even if it is on my USB stick. Anyway the recipe for quiche in the MACS is sort of okay, that is if you are feeding hundreds like we were and wanted to make it go further, to be fair though had we made quiches like the ones in the photo we would have used a lot of the DMR (Daily messing rate) in one meal, so to make it cheaper we used to add tinned milk and water to the egg mixture to make it stretch out. You can tell if it was made with milk as when you cut into it you can see it as the egg custard texture with less cheese to cut the cost and more salt to give it taste, just like you buy in the supermarkets. I can honestly tell you I have tried numerous recipes for making quiche mostly with bad finished results both in taste and texture, this is my concoction and it works and apart from the pastry it is mostly guesswork. The ingredients for this are so simple and there is no weighing up, the pastry for this is short crust as you will see, the idea is to get the pastry as paper thin as possible to line the moulds, what you don't want is a pork pie crust if you see what I mean. Remember this pastry is to hold the filling without it leaking, when it is cooked you have the delicate pastry crust holding loads of the filling, once you have tasted it you won't want to buy the supermarket quiche again. I used six Ramekin dishes mainly for presentation purposes for this book, normally I would do mine in flan rings or trays, plus my neighbors and family know that I am doing a cook book and it is easier to share the food out amongst them. You can use a flan dish or a baking tin, or if you want you can even use the tinfoil containers that you get your chinese in, all you have to remember is to judge the ingredients carefully so you have enough filling. Also if you make a deeper one say one to two inches make sure you cook it at a lower temparuture for longer otherwise it will souffle and overcook and make the texture dry. Once you have your dishes grease them with some butter or oil and get ready to put it all together.

*****

Short crust pastry.

11

Plain flour 6oz

Butter 1 ½ oz.

Lard 1 ½ oz

Water to bind.

The filling.

Eggs – eight to ten more if you use a bigger dish

Onion – One chopped more if you want

Grated cheese - As much as you like or need. (Save some grated cheese)

Salt – Pinch

Water – A small amount

Put the flour in a bowl with the butter, lard and a pinch of salt then rub it in with your fingers, have a small amount of water in a jug ready and mix into the flour very slowly with a fork till the mixture comes together and leaves the side of the bowl clean, be careful don't add too much water. Once mixed it will be like a soft dough, that's how you want it. Divide into six and roll each piece out using flour, this is probably the hardest part as you need to roll it paper thin like filo pastry as shown in the photo.

***

If you are making the quiche in a flan dish then you will just need to roll the whole lot out. Place the rolled pieces over the dishes and gently press them into the sides ensuring there are no air pockets just prick it with the sharp knife and the air will come out just make sure you press the pastry again to seal.

Trim off with a knife as shown. That is the hard part done. Put the chopped onions in a dish with a bit of butter then wrap fast and cook in microwave for three minutes, this will cook and soften them. You can cook them gently on the stove if you wish but they don't want browning at all, don't be tempted to put the onions in the quiche raw as they will give it a bitter taste when cooked. Put the cheese, Eggs, Onions and a pinch of salt in the bowl as shown, you can use what ever cheese you like it is up to you. Mix it all together and note there is no milk in this recipe. Carefully spoon the mixture into the dishes filling each one, then put the rest of the grated cheese on top. Put the quiches in the centre of a pre heated oven about 100 to 150 they will take about 25 to 30 minutes, keep your eye on them. If you think they are browning too fast turn the oven down. Sometimes it is better to start with a slightly cooler oven.

After about 30 minutes they should be golden brown gently press the tops with your finger, if they are firm they are ready. Sometimes you can cook them too fast so the secret is to cook them gently. As soon as they come out of the oven you will want to eat these while they are hot and they smell delicious, perfect with a salad. If you wish you can add some ham, cooked bacon or cooked mushrooms to the mix it is entirely up to you. Experiment with different ingredients that you may like and build your own quiche, just remember don't be tempted to use milk.

MEAT FREE SCOTCH EGG

Before I go into the recipe for these, I just want to mention the compo sausage it was without a shadow of doubt one of the squaddies favourite compo items, always popular with the tank crews. There wasn't a great deal we could do with these sausages on exercise apart from breakfast, maybe lunch time we could make sausage rolls, or maybe we would serve them up in gravy with onions or sometimes chop them if we were making a savoury rice. Lefty Wright was one of the cooks I worked with at the time, he was a natural when it came to compo I remember once he put the compo sausage in a baking tray covered them with fried onions then topped it all with POM the compo mashed potato, before putting it in the oven he sprinkled with grated cheese possessed which was our name for processed cheese, basically it was a sausage and mash baked in the oven but it was something different. Lefty was a very inventive chef especially when we were on exercise, his problem was he was always in trouble especially back in barracks. One day he was on duty cook, now the duty cook would normally get finished about 9pm after all the guard were fed and the preparation for the following day were done, Lefty was on earlys the next morning and would have to be back in at 5am to cook breakfast for the regiment. But it didn't stop him going out on the piss that night when he finished his duty, so he decided to make it easier by getting the beans and

14

tomatoes into the steamer in serving trays, this was a normal practice by all of us so that when you came in the following morning they were hot and ready for the hot plate, Lefty cracked 160 eggs for the scrambled egg and decided to put them in the steamer too. The next morning Lefty arrived for his earlys in a drunken stupor and as you can imagine the eggs were totally ruined, they were a green discoloured solid block stuck firmly in the serving tray. Lefty wasn't perturbed by this so he got a whisk and poured some canned evaporated milk in, then he broke the solid egg mass up by whisking vigorously, apparently it looked and smelled disgusting it was totally inedible, even the pigs in the piggery would have turned their noses up, but Lefty in his wisdom put it out for breakfast and sprinkled parsley on top hoping to disguise the way it looked. Complaints soon got back to the master chef who went ballistic when he found out leaving Lefty in the deep shit for serving it up, he ended up on a charge and got seven days ROPs (Restriction of privileges). If he had thrown it away in the first place and told the master chef, he had burnt it, Lefty would have most likely got of lightly.

Seedy Simpson the sex mad cook was the master story teller and once told us about a cook he had gone through training with, then to Seedy's horror they both ended up posted to the same unit which was with the 17th/21st Lancers (Boneheads) his name was Gopper Price, He was called Gopper because of his personal hygiene which was gopping or minging. Seedy told us that during training Gopper stunk fucking awful and he would very rarely have a bath. They once had a locker inspection and Gopper's kit was minging, it was so bad that the drill corporal started gipping which resulted in a blanket punishment for all the squad, this is where everyone gets punished for one person in the hope that the rest of them will bring the offender in line. Not Gopper he came back pissed one weekend and went in the toilets and fell asleep on the bog with his trousers up pissing and shitting himself. That was the final straw and the lads got Gopper's towels from his filthy locker and went into the washrooms armed with bass brooms and ajax and woke him up. In surprise he grabbed the towels and tried to clean himself. The squad grabbed him and led him to the shower where they stripped him naked, the smell was putrid as they threw him and his clothes in the shower and scrubbed him with the brooms and ajax, this was known as a regimental bath, apparently the screams could be heard in the next block. When the squad had scrubbed him Gopper was red raw as he made his way back to the bog where he was asleep earlier, then he picked up the minging towel and dried himself with it, that was Gopper all over, like Lefty Wright, Gopper was forever in trouble. Seedy continued to tell us that Gopper was always trying to work his ticket (Get out of the army) anyway he didn't turn up for work one morning and the master chef told Seedy to go and find him. Seedy found him in his room pissed out of his brain drinking straight Asbach (Brandy) out of the bottle, he told Seedy to fuck off and bring the RSM. The bonehead RSM arrived with the RP staff, Gopper started trying to caress the RSM saying he had always liked him in a very special way, needless to say the RP staff grabbed hold of Gopper before he could even touch the RSM and he was marched to the clink within seconds

15

(mind your fingers). To Gopper's dismay he got 14 days detention and soldier on.

Back to the compo sausage I myself never tried or thought to make scotch eggs with these sausages but if I could get hold of a can today, I would give it a go with the help of a blender, breadcrumbs and eggs, I would love to try it just to say I made scotch eggs out of compo sausage.

This is another of my recent recipes which I found on the internet and made it my own, no way am I vegan or vegetarian I have always liked my meat and the thought of a scotch egg being made without sausage meat was a big no for me. I remember in the cookhouse we would have loads of old bread which we would grind through a sieve into breadcrumbs and add them to the sausage meat to boost the portions. We would mix it all on the Hobart machine with eggs to bind it, what we had was 10% sausage meat and 90% breadcrumbs, with just the sausage meat we would have made about 20 scotch eggs so with the addition of the bread we could boost that up to 100, that was military portion control at its best. I can remember we would all form a line, one cook would shape the meat mix putting the boiled egg in and sealing it, then pass it on to the flour man who would roll it about and pass it on for egg washing and finally the last person would be bread crumbing them before they went into the deep fryer, happy days. I have to confess that in the past I have brought them from the supermarket myself, dry horrible cardboard things and if you shake them you can hear the egg rattling inside. These Linda McCartney sausages are very similar in texture to the compo sausage but not taste, therefore you have to put the flavour into them, my wife asked me to make them and with a bit of simple tweaking from the original recipe I came up with these and you can hardly tell the difference.

*****

One packet of 6 Linda McCartney vegetarian sausage

Two boiled eggs shelled

One red or white onion, both if you want

Small knob of butter

Two Ryvita biscuits crushed

Salt and black pepper

*****

These scotch eggs are unique as you don't need egg yolks to bind them, simply chop the onions and put in a bowl with the butter, cling film and microwave for about 3 minutes till soft. Meanwhile put the sausage in a bowl add salt and black pepper, once the onions are cooked and cooled add them to the sausage and mix and bind everything together, these six sausages will make two scotch eggs. Split the mixture and form into patty's place an egg in the centre and carefully wrap the meat around making sure to seal it properly, imagine you have a tennis ball in your palm passing it from hand to hand. Finally drop it in the crushed Ryvita and cover with the crumbs. You can still egg and bread crumb if you wish it is up to you. Place on a baking tray in the oven about 150 for about 35 to 40 minutes till golden but again keep your eye on them don't over brown them. Once cooked simply cut in half and serve up we like a salad with ours, the kids like chips and beans with theirs. There you are simple and easy and you can prepare them in advance.

EASY JAM SPONGE PUDDING

When we were kids the only time apart from school dinners that we got a pudding in our house was at weekends at Sunday dinner. My mother used to buy those Heinz tinned sponges they were in a larger than normal can and she used to drop the can into boiling water to heat it. I can remember when she took the can out and it was bulging due to the pressure, she would get the tin opener ready to open it and throw a cloth over just before she punctured the tin, there was a whoosh as the pressurised air escaped from under the towel, then she would portion it into eight small wedges and we had it with custard. It was only a few spoonful's each but for us it was a treat.

As a young cook working in a military kitchen, I would weigh the mix up in the morning using the MACs recipe. We never got self-rising flour in the cookhouse, it was always plain probably because it was cheaper, so we would have to add the baking powder to the mix separately. Once the mix was complete, we would pour it into the long metal sleeves and put them in the steamers about mid-day and literally forget about them till tea time. The beauty of the MACs recipe is it could be adapted to any type of sponge you needed, jam, treacle, lemon, orange, ginger, spotted dick anything you wanted. When we were out on exercise, I never realized that a sponge could be made from compo, mainly because of the laborious mixing that it involved. Back in the barracks we had the luxury of industrial electric mixers or "Hobarts" as we called them. My old friend the sex mad Seedy Simpson would have a go at

18

anything and I am not just talking about women, the compo margarine and sugar were plentiful and we had the normal issue of eggs and flour. I have to take my hat off to Seedy. Once he got a task on his mind, he would persevere until he finished it including women. He was once knocking a married woman off who lived in the next married quarter block to him and his wife. The husband of his fancy piece was away on exercise but came back unexpectedly Apparently in a panic she threw Seedy's clothes out of the bedroom window and they got snagged in a tree, Seedy was seen clambering down the drain pipe with one shoe on with just his undies and a shirt which was inside out It was the middle of winter and Seedy was freezing his bollocks off. Seedy made his way home to his wife who had been concerned of his whereabouts asking him why he was half naked with one shoe, he casually told her he had been in the camp squadron bar and the lads had given him his initiation test stripping him naked in the process. I think sometimes his wife was blind to the things he did, either that or she was very dumb, initiation tests were just horseplay and if they happened. It normally took place when you first joined a regiment and Seedy had been with us over two years. When he had a few beers Seedy would often tell us stuff that would have us rolling about laughing.

The hard part about doing this sponge on exercise was mixing the sugar and margarine together with a wooden spoon it was even harder with a whisk. I remember Seedy was stood for ages creaming the sugar and axle grease compo marge together with a wooden spoon holding the bowl close to his stomach for a better grip making suggestive movements with the spoon as he panted and moaned, he had us all in stitches with his sexual innuendos, then he added the eggs one by one and finally the flour and baking powder then he would put the mix in the 20x10x2, ready for the field oven, it didn't rise as good as Seedy expected and he was a bit disappointed having put all that hand work into it.

'What a fucking waste,' he said wiping the sweat from his forehead and rubbing his crotch, 'I could have used all that hand energy for something else.'

Once again, we were all pissing ourselves laughing.

However, it wasn't a bad attempt for an experiment, Seedy covered the sponge with compo jam and dished it up with custard made with water and the dried milk, the troops ate the lot. Because of all the hard work in the mixing of this compo concoction I neither saw Seedy or anyone else for that matter do it again on exercise. To be fair to Seedy, I once tried it in the barracks when I was in the pastry department, using the same recipe and compo marge which we had an abundance of from past exercises, but I did it on the Hobart machine, I put the mix into the steamer and it turned out okay, so Seedy was on the right track.

This recipe I have got for the above photos is easy and it can be cooked in the oven. I don't do a lot of puddings these days since I retired but I used this recipe regularly especially for the diabetics where I worked. It was a quick alternative to the normal pudding, I just used sweet and low in the place of sugar. This recipe takes me about 10 minutes including the three-minute cooking time and you don't even have to turn the oven on, give it a try you will be surprised.

*****

For two portions.

Butter 2oz

Sugar 2oz

S R Flour 2oz

Milk 2 tablespoons

Egg 1

Jam or treacle or lemon curd-one large tablespoon full

Vanilla essence to flavour

For more portions just double up

*****

Grease the Ramekin dishes or whatever you are going to use. Ensure they are okay for the microwave. Next put a heaped tablespoon of jam into the dishes and spread so it covers the bottom. Put all the ingredients in a bowl as shown above. Yes! Just throw them all together and mix thoroughly using a spoon or fork. Make sure everything is mixed to a smooth thick batter then share it into the Ramekin dishes, cling film securely and put in the microwave for three minutes. You will see them rise as they cook just leave them till the time is up. Once cooked they should be firm. Leave them for a few minutes with the cling film on and be careful they will be hot. Turn them out and serve with custard I just get a tin of custard and put it in a jug and microwave it just as cheap and saves messing about. An easy pudding, so go on give it a try the kids will love it, later in this book I will show you a simple sticky toffee pudding also done in the microwave or the oven.

CHICKEN KEBAB

This is one of the few non compo related items in this book easy to make and perfect for barbeques. When we used to do cocktail parties years ago in the officer's mess, we would have to do these on a smaller scale using cocktail sticks, by the time we had done about five hundred we were well and truly pissed off. Trust me they were a pain in the arse. As well as these we would have to do hundreds of different canapes, mini tartlets and side dips. Luckily, we also had access to some of the officer's wine Chateauneuf du pape for some reason always sticks in my mind to keep us sane and pissed while we were preparing these tedious delicacies.

When we were on exercise on Soltau west Germany all the regiment would have at least one weekend where they would park all their tanks and vehicles up at the edge of Reinselen camp so they could use the showers and ablutions and generally get everything cleaned up and in order again ready for the following Monday when the exercise would continue. I remember the sink in the washrooms and I say sink with no plural, it was a long stone trough with taps every few feet and one long mirror. You pressed the top of the tap and the water would come out for about 30 seconds so by the time you were in mid wash the bloody thing turned itself off and you had to repeat the process. The showers were exactly the same they were huge wet rooms with about sixty showerheads. Once again you pressed the chrome button and the water would flow. As soon as you got lathered up the water turned itself off and you had to

21

repeat the process until you finished your shower. The shower floor after each of the five squadrons of greasy dirty troops had been through was like a quagmire of mud and slime, this would have to be cleaned thoroughly by a fatigue party from each squadron when they had finished, under the watchful eye of the RQMS (Regimental Quartermaster Sergeant). One thing about coming in to the shower block was the toilets and the luxury of not going into a wood with a shovel, I won't go into detail but like I said in the (Forward) at the beginning the compo was good stuff. The best thing though was the graffiti on the toilet walls absolutely brilliant funny stuff that would have you sat there in stitches reading the filthy sexual jokes and piss taking story's, Seedy Simpson would often spend hours in there with his black marker pen and a copy of Fiesta. I have even known people change toilets so they can read more of the graffiti. I always remember one phrase that I saw and it tickles me to this day. "Please flush twice it is a fucking long way to the cookhouse" brilliant.

Once all the troops were cleaned up it was time for the highlight of the exercise "The squadron smokers". Bonfires would be built and the squadron SQMS would ensure there was plenty of beer and cigs, I would be sent to the local butchers to get the meat for the barbeque, the whole squadron would chip in a few deutschemarks each for this, or it would come out of the squadron funds. As well as bratwurst and burgers I would get chicken, pork, beef steak and make kebabs for the smoker. For my civilian friends these smokers were some of the best nights that I can remember, they were the ultimate night out on the lash, better than anything we did back in barracks and unless you have experienced them yourselves you don't know what you missed. After the food and copious amounts of beer the dangerous games of fire dancing would begin, like the red Indians in the movies the troops would be dancing quickly over the burning embers and I mean quickly, some of them were tied to trees and covered in Swarfega, one year we even had a crucifixion. I remember once they tied a rope from tree to tree which hung precariously over the fire and then you would see pissed up squaddies doing the death slide to the other side, one by one as the night wore on people would drift away to their bivis and sleeping bags leaving only the diehard's around the dying fire singing and generally acting the goat, great nights and great memories.

These kebabs are quick and easy to make, if you are not keen on chicken you could use steak, lamb, pork or any meat you fancy, just make sure you get a decent cut of meat and don't go buying the readymade ones they are more expensive and homemade ones are so much better. The sweet chilli sauce compliments them perfectly and can be purchased from Lidl. You can grill these to colour them, then finish in the oven, I prefer to use the George Foreman which gives them a lovely charred effect, I keep spraying mine with a fry light spray. Once they are cooked you can serve them with salad as above or rice or noodles

*****

For four kebabs

Three or four chicken breasts cut into chunks

Assorted peppers

Red or white Onions

Whole mushrooms with the stalk remove

Four skewers

Salt, pepper and any flavouring seasoning of your choice I used an Italian one

*****

Start with a piece of chicken then alternate with each of the vegetables until you fill the stick. Keep them tightly together and get as much on as you can. Once you have completed them season well and they are ready for cooking. Like some of my other recipes you can pre prepare these the day before cover them with cling film and pop in the fridge. You can flavour these to your liking. Fresh garlic, ginger ect. Have a look in the supermarket spices and flavourings and indulge yourself. Don't stick to a recipe format let your imagination go.

SAUSAGE PASTA

When I first started doing this recipe, I used to cook the sausages let them cool then chop them up and put them in the sauce last. This recipe stemmed from a Sainsburys advert where Jamie Oliver used to cook meals for four for under a fiver. The original recipe that he did was meat balls (beef) garlic, tinned chopped tomatoes, spaghetti, grated cheese, onions and frozen peas. It was very nice too and at the time we had it about twice a week till we got fed up of it. Last year I decided to resurrect it but with a slight difference I would use sausage meat instead. You can use whatever sausage you like, we prefer Cumberland, if you prefer pasta shells instead of spaghetti just go ahead there are no rules in my cooking. What I love about this is the cooking time, you can put it in the slow cooker and forget about it, the pasta can be cooked earlier and the beauty is you can set the slow cooker on low before you go to work or go out for the day, when you get home all you have to do is mix the spaghetti and peas into the sausage leave for ten minutes to heat through then serve sprinkled with grated cheese.

As I said the compo sausage on manoeuvres were very popular with the troops and if we did manage to be lucky enough to have any left over from breakfast we would thinly slice them and fry them with a few onions, field mushrooms and finely diced luncheon meat we would then add water with the

24

compo dried rice it was similar to a poor man's risotto. If we were lucky, we may have acquired some soya sauce, it was our way of using the leftovers up and doing something different. However, it was very rare there were any left after breakfast as they were so popular. Breakfast on exercise was the best meal of the day by far, consisting of fried eggs, sausage, bacon grill, bacon burgers, fried bread and not forgetting the beans, most of this could be prepared the night before apart from the baked beans which would be heated in the tins and boiled in the water the following morning. So, we would put them in the six-gallon container in the cold water and ready them for the burner stand the next day, it was always better to do it this way because if we put them straight on the cooker they would burn very quickly with the intense heat. A new young cook had arrived Pete Riley who we named Mavis; the master chef had asked Seedy to take Mavis under his wing as it was his first exercise in the field. When doing the breakfast prep Seedy told Mavis to put the baked beans in the water in the six-gallon container, this is a classic amongst us cooks. Mavis opened the beans and put them in the cold water. The next morning Mavis was lighting the burners to cook breakfast.

'Mavis? What the fuck have you done here?' screamed Seedy.

What do you mean?' he said.

'I told you to put the fucking beans in cold water!'

'I did Seedy,' said Mavis.

'Not literally you fucking idiot I meant the tins, look at the state of them!'

The beans were now floating in the cold water, the water was a thin coloured brine like something in a wash tub, Seedy was always the man of the moment with his cowboy methods and after giving poor Mavis a bollocking he strained most of the water off the beans then brought them to the boil on the burner and thickened the watery bean liquid with cornflour it looked disgusting but Seedy still put them on for breakfast, unbelievably most of it went with just a few complaints from the troops, in response Seedy told them that the MOD (Ministry of defence) had sent a bad compo batch hehe.

*****

For four people

One packet of sausages.

One chopped onion.

One punnet of button mushrooms or normal ones sliced.

One full bulb of garlic crushed depending how much you like it.

One jar of bolognaise sauce. (Dolmio or similar)

25

Spaghetti.

Mug full of frozen garden peas.

Salt and pepper as required.

Oil for frying or use the fry light spray.

*****

Separate the eight sausage then one at a time pull the meat out of the skin with your fingers you should have four pieces of meat per sausage and a total of twenty-four when you have done them all. Don't worry if they are not perfect in shape it doesn't matter, seal them in a pan with a drop of oil as shown above. Once they are sealed add the onions, mushroom and garlic and cook through gently. Put everything into the slow cooker and cover with the sauce give it a quick stir then put the lid on and forget it. The spaghetti can be cooked in advance it just needs adding to the sausage with the peas ten minutes before you eat it, serve onto dish and sprinkle with plenty grated cheese. I have left the sausage in the sauce on low slow cook for six hours so don't worry it will be fine.

SIMPLE ROAST CHICKEN

I put roast chicken on as one of my top favourites because every time I see a cooked half chicken I think of this little story.

Years ago, in Fallinbostel west Germany I was told there were only two or three officers in for the evening meal as the majority of them had gone to a barbeque. That was a green light for me to go to the local German pub and get pissed. I lost track of time and realized I still had dinner to cook so I ordered chicken and chips three times and staggered back to the officer's mess. Once there the waiter was panicking as to where I was and what I was doing for dinner, so I told him not to worry as I got three plates put the chicken and chips on with a bit of salad garnish and I opened a tin of fruit salad. I then went back to the pub with the duty waiter looking on at me in astonishment. Monday morning came and I asked the waiter if they enjoyed their dinner on Saturday as I was a bit worried that I would be in the shit for it. 'Yes, they did, 'he replied. Relieved at that I went to see the mess accountant and gave him the receipt for the chicken and chips and I got my money back, that's a classic and the amount of times I have told people this always gets a laugh. The nearest thing to roast chicken on exercise though was Wolfgang's bratty van who would find us no matter where we were or how bad the weather was, he was a welcome sight for us squaddies on those winter exercises and his bratwurst and senf was top spot.

These days it is quicker to go to the Asda and get a cooked roast chicken than do it at home, it costs about six quid for this, however I still have the rest of the dinner to prepare including the stuffing so when I have done I have spent a tenner for the two of us, not a lot of money but a bit lazy on my behalf plus neither me or Mandy are very keen on the leg meat which normally goes to the family dog. This roast chicken is quick and simple the stuffing is a combination of paxo, freshly chopped onion and a couple of Linda McCartney sausage.

*****

For four people.

Chicken breast x 4.

One cupful of paxo stuffing made up with boiling water.

One onion chopped and sweated off, either on the stove or in the microwave.

Linda McCartney sausage x 2.

Salt and pepper.

Light fry spray.

Put the chicken fillets on a baking tray and season both sides with salt and pepper, spray with the oil. Make the batch of paxo with boiling water and put in bowl with the sweated onions and Sausage. Mash it all together and form into four pieces and place on the chicken, cook in the oven about 150 for 25 to 30 minutes and coloured. Let it rest then carve the breasts and place on serving dish with the stuffing add the juices from the roasting tin let it cool and cover with cling film or plate up if you are eating it straight away. Simple all done and ready to be reheated.

MARS BAR CORNFLAKE BUNS

What the hell am I doing putting cornflake buns in my cook book? I hear you say, well let's have a break from compo and I will tell you that cornflake buns were the first thing I ever made when I did cookery at my secondary school in the mid-1960s. All the other boys would go off to their woodwork or metal work lessons and I would go with the girls to cookery class, it was called domestic science in those days. A lot of the boys used to take the piss out of me at break times but deep down I knew that a lot of them were just jealous because I was in the same classroom as Andrea Reynolds. Now Andrea was a bit of a girl and she seemed to spend a lot of time behind the bike sheds in fact she spent more time in them than the bikes. The lads would give me notes to give to her, I had a peek at these notes and they were sexually suggestive and disgusting, at the bottom of each note were small symbols which were a clue to Andrea as to who the sender was, like a fool I took them into the class with me, at the first opportunity I would pass them on to her. This particular day we were making cornflake buns and with all my ingredients ready I passed the notes to Andrea who was stood next to me. She read them with a smile on her face.

'What's that you just gave to Andrea, Michael?' said Miss Fox the teacher.

I grabbed the notes from Andrea and stuffed them back in my pocket.

'Give them here!' said Miss Fox.

I put my hand in my pocket again and peeled one of the notes out and reluctantly I gave it to the teacher and she opened it up and after a few seconds she turned bright red.'

'Disgusting!' she said, 'Empty your pockets out right now!'

I put the rest of the notes on the table and she read them one by one, all the girls were giggling and tittering at my predicament, Miss Fox put the notes in her cardigan pocket.

'I often wondered why you wanted to come in this class Michael Collins and now I know why, these notes are depraved and you should be ashamed of yourself, you will come with me at once to the headmaster.'

She was right what she said, the notes were short but very sexually explicit.

'But Miss,' I pleaded.

'Follow me!' she said, 'I don't want to hear your feeble excuses.'

She told me to wait outside while she went in the headmaster's office, I could hear her showing and telling him about the notes in a distressed voice.

'The little pervert!' he shouted, 'Send the wretched boy in here immediately!'

No matter how I tried to explain the headmaster was having none of it.

'But sir,' I pleaded, 'The notes are all in different handwriting.'

He looked at them again.

'Mmm,' he said, 'But that proves nothing, plus there are no names or initials!'

I was in the shit and the symbols at the bottom of each note meant nothing. It would probably have been more trouble for him to investigate and bring the real culprits to justice, so he made an example of me. I was given the cane by the headmaster and banned from the school kitchens I was sent back to the woodwork and metalwork class to the cheers and whoops from the rest of my class mates. However, after the note incident we did see the headmaster on occasion walking past the bike sheds, I think he knew there was something in my wild story and decided to investigate it himself, but it all came to nothing.

We have all made these little cakes at one time or another and I had to put them in this book because of the story behind them, however I have put a twist to them to make them more cheffy and I have used mars bars.

*****

Makes twelve smaller buns or eight larger ones.

Eight mars bars, save two for the decoration.

Butter 50g

Cornflakes 100g

White chocolate for decoration(optional)

*****

Melt the butter over a pan of water as shown, chop six of the mars bars and add them to the butter, stir till you get a smooth toffee sauce consistency.

Add the sauce to the cornflakes and stir in till all the flakes are coated.

Using two dessert spoons put the mixture into the bun cases pile em up.

Chop the remaining mars bars into slices and decorate the tops as shown in the photo, put the cakes in the fridge.

Meanwhile melt the white chocolate in the glass bowl, once the cakes have set you can either pipe the white chocolate with a fine piping tube like they use on icing cakes or just drizzle it over using a teaspoon.

Get the kids to help you make them. Oh! and they taste delicious and I am sure that Andrea Reynolds would be proud of me, I often wonder if she recognised the little note, I sent her that day.

APPLE PIE

One of the compo packs had tins of apple pudding, it had a suet like pastry around it very similar to the compo steak and kidney pudding which I will explain later in this book. We would open both ends of the tin so we could push the pudding out then cut them in half and place in the 20x10x2 tray we would then make a custard with the compo dried milk and water to cover the puddings before we put them in the oven. The texture as I remember was similar to a jam roly poly but with apple, it was spot on and very filling.

This little luxury apple pie is made with Pink Lady apples and a rich sweet pastry

*****

Sweet pastry.

Plain flour 8oz

Butter 4oz

Icing sugar 3oz

One egg

*****

Simply put it all in the processer and it should all come together, if it's a bit dry add water but be careful just a little drop at a time. Cover with cling film and put in the fridge to rest for half an hour.

I remember when we were on exercise especially the big FTX ones in Germany we would be camped out on farms and the German farmers were crazy about the army composite rations, they also knew it was first class stuff which was designed to give a soldier more than his daily calorie intake, the farmers loved it especially the cheese and jams that were in abundance and it was brilliant barter power when we were on exercise in the field. We would swap it for vegetables, eggs, fresh milk, cream which when we were away from camp were luxury items. One of the other luxuries of been near a farmhouse if we were lucky was an outside toilet that the farmer would allow us to use in exchange for our compo, it was so much better than slinking into the woods with a shovel in one hand and a bog roll in the other. Also, if the farmer let us use his barn for sleeping in it was an added bonus it was so much better laying our sleeping bags out on the hay in a dry barn. I remember one year we were static on a farm for a few days and there was a pub about 100 metres down the road, Our QM (Quartermaster) at the time went there to do a recce, when he came back he told us that the German landlord said it would be okay for us to use the toilet providing we had a drink. Anyway, the QM warned us, only one drink each when we go into the bar then go and do your business, drink up and return here. So, when me and Seedy went to the pub we ordered 1.4 litre steins each hehe, happy days, well the QM did say only one drink each. One particular day a farmer brought us a sack full of apples (talk about enough to feed an army), so many we didn't know what to do with them, we had plenty flour, sugar and compo margarine so we made big trays of apple pie which lasted us for days.

*****

For four pies.

Apples (five or 6) I used pink ladies use whatever you want.

Caster sugar four tablespoons.

Cinnamon.

Juice of one lime or lemon and the zest. (optional)

*****

Peel and quarter the apples chop into small chunks and place in glass dish add the sugar and the only liquid you need is the lime juice. Cling film and microwave for five minutes or till soft, let it cool then strain off the surplus liquid needs to be dry as possible, add the zest stir and put back in the fridge.

Take the pastry out you made earlier and cut into eight pieces Roll each piece out and gently press it into the mould and up the sides, if you accidently press too hard just get a bit of pastry and patch it up, if you are doing a flan do the same thing. Sweet pastry is delicate but it is also flexible, you could use short pastry instead which is easier to handle that is entirely up to you, I think the sweet pastry gives a nice finish which is similar to shortbread.

Share the apple out in each one, slight dampen the edges of the pastry then roll the last four pieces for the top, press down gently and with a sharp knife trim the pastry, don't throw the pastry away make some jam tarts or something. Crimp the edges with the tip of knife as above and prick the tops twice with a cocktail stick. Very lightly and sparingly brush with a drop of cold water and sprinkle with a bit of sugar. Cook about 140 to 150 nice and steady till golden about 35 to 40 minutes, let cool then turn out while still warm the bottoms should be cooked leave on a rack then fridge for a few hours. Decorate as you wish, I have done mine a bit fancy, you could have custard or just double cream. Use what moulds or flan tins you feel comfortable with, the moulds I am using are specifically for this book and presentation purposes. If you are making larger pies you may need to double up on the pastry and apples, just remember if you are making sweet pastry it needs to be kept in the fridge until you use it. And if you want an easy life do the apples the same as above, place in a glass dish, then mix together and microwave till soft.

Crumble mix

8oz plain flour.

4oz best butter.

3oz of brown or white sugar.

Put the crumble on top. Delicious either way but so much better with fresh apples and homemade, time I went for a stein.

CHEESE AND ONION PANCAKES

Before I go into these pancakes let me tell you about some more of the equipment that we used in the field kitchen.

One of the most scariest things in my life was when I was 17 years old and I was stuck sixty foot up in the air on the Paras trainasium when I was doing my preliminary tests to become a would be paratrooper in Aldershot, the sheer horror of that experience and my fear of heights still haunts me to this day, the para story is in my first book. My close second scariest moment of all was lighting the M67 immersion heater which we used in the field for boiling hot water for the troops to wash in. the M67 sounds like some kind of ammunition or a bomb (see photo below), in actual fact in the wrong hands it was a fucking bomb and I hated lighting it. The M67 you see in the photo would be put in a galvanised dustbin like container and filled with water, the chimney spout was about eight foot in height. The round fuel tank was filled with petrol and on top of this tank was an air release valve, underneath was a small tap for the petrol. Before you lit it there was a little lever that brought a little container cup out of the flue which would end up under the petrol tap. You would turn the tap and fill this cup then light it and spring it back into the flue to heat it up so it would draw the air this took a few minutes; it was imperative that you did this. Once the flue was hot you would then open the air valve and then the petrol tap to start it dripping at the same time lighting it, after a few drips turn the tap off and wait for the petrol to draw in the bottom of the heater, then you would turn the tap on again with a very slow drip and it would hopefully start the heating process. Sounds horrendous doesn't it? and it is. I once put the tap on too fast and when I lit it the whole thing just exploded into flames, black soot was everywhere as the top of the flue accelerated upwards like a rocket, I couldn't get my hand back to turn the tap off as it was too hot, so there was only one option left and that wasn't in the instructions, fucking run! Luckily, I had my beret on at the time but my eyebrows had gone,

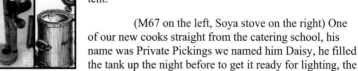

I looked like a panda as I made my way to the medical tent.

(M67 on the left, Soya stove on the right) One of our new cooks straight from the catering school, his name was Private Pickings we named him Daisy, he filled the tank up the night before to get it ready for lighting, the next morning he went to light it without heating the flue up, he let the petrol drip into the bottom too fast then has he threw a match in, the whoosh of the petrol exploding like a mortar being fired and threw Daisy backwards into the side of the water bowser we were preparing breakfast when we heard the bang and were soon on the scene, Daisy was still clutching the book of white burnt matches, his face was black and he had tufts of burnt hair on his head, it looked like something out of the road runner cartoon, as serious as it was we were trying our hardest not to laugh. He had to be taken to the medical centre in Hohne for his facial burns. Not many people were successful with these things including me, the lighting was a painstaking process and the instructions needed to be read thoroughly, if you google M67 immersion heater and you can see one being lit. The guard were eventually detailed to light these things up before the cooks got up on a morning then we could just concentrate on our number one burner. Very often we would be laying in our sleeping bags at 4am in the morning and hear booms and explosions followed by "fucking hell" as the guard were blowing themselves up. Private Daisy Pickings spent a few days in hospital, when he finally came back to the barracks after the exercise he looked like a snake with no eyebrows and most of his hair missing with red blotches all over his face, he was a lucky man.

Back to the pancakes when I was working full time, I used to love making them for the residents either sweet or savoury, to prepare for this I would always make them the day before especially as we neared Shrove Tuesday. I would stand at the stove for over an hour making these with a large container of batter mix and a couple of frying pans, I would stack them on top of each other ready for the next day when I would prepare them. I used to like doing Crepes Normandie where I would fill them with apple, lemon, sugar and cinnamon I used to tray them all up and mask them with golden syrup before warming them in the oven, served up with thick double cream, delicious and no good for the waist line. Of course, there are the traditional flavours of orange and lemon I have tried them with cherries, honey, blueberries, bananas even chocolate. I also liked making savoury ones like chicken and mushroom in a bechamel sauce (White sauce) which I would serve out as a lunch choice. I have stuffed them with cheese and ham in a thick sauce, then egg and breadcrumb them before deep frying them. Corned beef hash was one of my favourite meals that my mother used to make when we were kids, she would ladle it on to a thick large pancake, the food of the gods and in the winter months me and Mandy still eat it regularly. On army exercises back in Germany it was very rare we would leave camp without a bag of flour and plenty eggs they were the main back up for the compo if we were cooking in the field and with them, we could work miracles. There were seven different compo packs at the time ABCDEFG all different menus, one in particular had chicken supreme, there were quite a few things we could do with this including pies and pasties, sometimes we would wash the sauce off in cold water and cook the meat in a batter served with the rice for sweet and sour, chicken supreme was also perfect for these pancakes.

*****

For four people.

One chopped onion.

Grated cheese as much as you like.

Plain flour 2oz.

Butter 2oz.

Milk.

Salt.

Drop of double cream

Pancake mix.

One level mug of plain flour.

One level mug of milk.

Two eggs

Salt.

Drop of water if needed.

Oil for frying.

*****

Put all the pancake ingredients together in a bowl and whisk until a smooth batter, double cream consistency, if you think it is too thick add a drop of water.

37

Put the onions in a microwaveable bowl, knob of butter, pinch of salt and cling film cook for three minutes till soft. Meanwhile make the white sauce (bechamel) put the butter in a pan on the heat, melt then stir in the flour to form the roux, add the milk slowly stirring all the time. You can buy the packet rubbish from the supermarket if you wish but this tastes so much better homemade. You are looking for a thick consistency like wall paper paste, if it is too thin it will leak from the pancake, let it cook for a minute keep stirring to cook the flour out. Add the cheese and cooked onion then stir in, once it as melted and combined add a drop of cream and a pinch of salt, after another good mix cover and allow to cool.

While it is cooling you can cook the pancakes, you can either use a smaller omelette type pan or like me a full size one. Heat the pan with a drop of oil then when it is hot add the pancake mix, not to thick and not too thin as in the photo, let it cook don't try to turn it too early, lift one of the edges slightly to check the colour underneath you need a light golden brown then you can flip it over using the egg slice or if you are confident you can toss it, Seedy was good at this hehe, that's the pancake by the way. Lay the pancakes out and put the cold filling in each one it should be nice and thick now, fold up as shown in the photos and place into a baking dish, sprinkle with grated cheese and a few slices of tomatoes you can either cook for about 25 minutes in the oven about 100 to 150, once again keep your eye on them they just need to be heated through, or better still put a couple on a plate and microwave for a minute or so, the kids love these with chips.

CRÈME BRULEE

Oh, my good lord if you are on a diet then don't make these, I made two and was nearly in tears when I gave them away to our next-door neighbours because me and Mandy are on strict diets.

Before I go into this recipe there is another piece of field equipment, I want to tell you about and that is the Soya Stove and unlike the M67 which came into use during the second world war, this stove goes back to world war one, plus it wasn't as dangerous. During the 1980s we used these for boiling water but more so for frying chips, however we didn't have to light a fire under them, we would place some bricks in front of the fire grate and stand the trusty number one burner on them which would blast the heat into the grate area. If we were on a big static exercise, we would fill the insert with fat or oil and blanch loads of fresh chunky chips for the troops, when lunch time came, we could brown all the blanched chips off quickly in the hot fat and I have to say they tasted lovely.

This is one of my favourite puddings and if it is on the menu when we go out for a meal, I often order it. Crème Brulee or burnt cream as it was known is a dessert that was made by accident or so I have read. The recipe goes back to 1691 believe it or not, it apparently started off as a cream pudding and the chef would use a branding iron with the coat of arms to decorate the top, when grills were finally invented the chef would put it under to brown it with sugar on, having forgot about it he returned to see that the sugar had caramelised giving it that lovely hard top that you have to crack with a teaspoon. I used to make it a lot when I worked in the officers mess, we used to have the big salamander grills so we could get the top caramelised quickly, these days I use a blow torch as shown in the photo, you can get them for a fiver if you want one. Have a go they are not difficult but require your attention while they are cooking, they need to be baked nice and slowly, I will explain.

For two people.

Double cream 350 ml.

Egg yolks 4.

Vanilla essence or a vanilla pod.

Caster sugar 2 x tablespoons

Two greased ramakin dishes and a baking tray to put them in.

Put the cream in a saucepan and bring to the boil steadily, don't let it burn.

Whisk the yolks, sugar and a drop of vanilla essence together thoroughly.

When the cream starts to boil pour it onto the yolks and sugar whisking all the time otherwise it will curdle. Once you have whisked it thoroughly strain the custard into a jug then share it between the ramakin moulds as this is my own recipe if you have another ramakin you may just get another depending how you fill them. I cooked these in a halogen oven on a rack as shown. Put them in the baking tray then put water in the tray, best to put the water in when they are in the oven. Oven temperature 160 turn it down to 140 after ten minutes or so, don't let them over brown or boil keep your eye on them, take about 25 to 30 minutes, touch the top of them they should have set like jelly texture if you know what I mean. Once cooked let them cool then put them in the fridge for four hours or overnight. Just before serving sprinkle with a bit of caster sugar and use the blow torch to brown them you will see the sugar caramelising and bubbling, now get them eaten before somebody else does.

MUSHROOM AND CREAM CHEESE PASTA

This recipe was given to me by a family member earlier this year and I have to say it is absolutely delicious. Poached flaked salmon was the main ingredient and it was lovely but I much prefer it with button mushrooms. It is another of those recipes where you can please yourself and experiment with your favourites maybe prawns, smoked haddock, ham, chicken, the best thing about this is the garlic and plenty of it. Very similar in richness to spaghetti Carbonara but without the cheese and bacon. It brings back memories of my time back in Switzerland in the late seventies where we had the regimental ski hut in the beautiful mountain village of Urnerboden. I will never forget the zig zagging road up the mountain from the village of Linthal known as the Klausenpasse, it was prone to avalanches and the winding roads leading upwards were like something out of a James Bond movie. Looking out from the window of the Bedford at the sheer drops below set my arsehole twitching and I was relieved to get to the top which took us into a valley towards Urnerboden. Although we were in the valley, we were only about half way up the Klausenpasse, from Urnerboden the road went upwards again and over the tops and down into the picturesque town of Altdorf the place where William Tell was supposedly born. As we looked up toward the mountain peaks, we could see the small avalanches forming as the local authorities would fire avalanche charges above the peaks to make them safe, unfortunately that week was to end

41

in disaster for us as three of our officers and one of our sergeants were killed in a mountain avalanche. This was one of the saddest times of my army career and I remember it vividly. In the Ski hut me and Lefty Wright had cooked dinner for the troops who were all sat quiet with their untouched plates in front of them, you could cut the atmosphere with a knife, the normal busy talking and laughing troops was gone as they just stared at their plates in silence. A helicopter had flown down from Fallingbostel with the CO (Commanding Officer) who had come to comfort and reassure us all, when I think of Switzerland it always reminds me of those young men that we lost on that fateful day.

The ski hut was across the road from the Wilhelm Tell hotel which was owned by Herr and Frau Marti and on an evening we would normally all flock into the hotel bar for our beer ration. After the tragedy of the avalanche I went back to see the Marti's a few times who always looked after me I remember the lovely pasta that she would cook it was called Aelplermagronin and it was delicious and consisted of potatoes, pasta, cheese, apple, onion, garlic, cream, butter. Frau Marti would make loads of it as it was very popular with the passing guests.

This recipe is very similar minus the apple and potato.

For two people

*****

Button mushrooms as many as you like.

Onion two chopped.

One full bulb of garlic.

Philadelphia cream cheese, one 380g pack

Pasta for two people cooked.

*****

Fry the onions garlic and mushrooms in oil, butter or fry light till cooked but don't over brown, at this stage the kitchen smells lovely.

Turn the heat down and put all the cream cheese in the pan and stir it in, if you think it is a little thick then add a drop of milk.

Add the pasta and heat through, serve it with salad or baked potato even chips if you want. This is really lovely and at the moment one of my favourite pasta meals.

BAUERNFRUHSTUCK

Back in the late 1970s in Fallingbostel West Germany I used to frequent a pub in the town called the Bauernstube, roughly translated in English as the farmers room. It was a cracking little German pub and I spent a lot of my wages in there. On my days off I would walk from the camp into Fallingbostel (I can assure you I didn't walk back) once in the Bauernstube you could smell the bacon and onions frying it was bliss, I would sit at the bar and order a Bauernfruhstuck. Now believe it or not I did these on zero hotel. This was the officers mess three-ton Bedford a mini kitchen with household cookers and penthouse which attached to the side for dining and the COs briefings. This vehicle went out on exercise with us all the time, but more about this when you get to the bread recipe.

I made these for the officer's lunch one day using the compo bacon grill, potatoes and I had acquired some onions from a local farmer for some compo jam and cheese. The RSM (Regimental Sergeant Major) at the time was always up at sparrow fart and would be the first person I saw on a morning when he came for his hot water to wash in. Once he had done, he would be out picking mushrooms in the fields mainly for his own breakfast which I cooked for him but he would always bring extra back for me to use. So with all my ingredients I was all set to cook Bauernfruhstuck for lunch, I didn't have a

43

frying pan as such it was a big black square tray which was as big as the stove top itself I would turn all four gases on and the tray would go on top similar to a griddle, I used this for the eggs at breakfast time as well. For this Bauernfruhstuck I would put the eggs into a bowl and whisk them, then I would use a ladle to put the mixture on the oiled tray I could get about four nice omelettes on this tray at one time. On the other stove would be the filling all sizzling away ready to fill the omelettes. There was always a way to do things no matter what conditions we worked in, we just adapted to the equipment we had and improvised.

When I came home on leave in the 70s and 80s the Collins family would be off on camping trips to the coast and the order of the day would be to get smoked bacon, onions, potatoes and eggs and after a night on the beer I would cook this for breakfast with plenty bread and best butter which set us up for the day.

I think my Bauernfruhstuck tastes exactly the same as the German version the only difference is, I cook the potatoes, bacon and onions separate and I cook the eggs like an omelette, sometimes I add mushrooms and cheese, oh! and not forgetting black pepper.

The German version is cooked in the frying pan altogether until brown then the eggs are added last, when it is done it resembles a Spanish omelette. It is still delicious and the black pepper gives it a lovely taste.

For two people.
*****

Eggs x 6
Baby potatoes cooked and sliced leave skins on.
One onion finely chopped.
Smoked bacon lardons or normal bacon chopped into strips.
Mushrooms a slack handful or as many as you like.
Oil for frying.
Salt and black pepper
Grated cheese (optional)
*****

First of all, put the frying pan on the stove and heat the oil, put the potatoes in to cook.

Meanwhile fry the lardons of in a large sauce pan till they are nice and brown, then add the onions and mushrooms and cook with the bacon. Don't forget to keep turning the potatoes you need these nice and golden add some salt and black pepper.

Once the potatoes are nicely browned put them onto the cooked Bacon, onions and mushrooms, clean the pan with kitchen paper and put as drop more oil in it, put half the eggs in and stir with a fork till they are almost set, stir the potato mix up in the other pan try not to break them up and put half the of it on the omelette, fold it over carefully and tip it onto the plate holding the pan by the handle, once it is on the plate garnish it up and it is done, this is the tricky bit as the filling tends to fall out and it just needs a bit of practice when you roll the omelette as in the photo. The German one is held by the eggs, maybe as a practice do it this way first. If you want more calories put some

44

grated cheese on the omelette before you roll it in the pan. Me and Mandy love this and we often have it for our evening dinner with a salad. I am a great lover of German food and there will be more to follow later in the meantime I am going to tuck into my Bauernfruhstuck. Danke Schon.

LEMON MERENGUE FLAN

As a young lad at the army catering school in Aldershot this was one of the first desserts I made, I remember first thing on a morning we would go in the classroom and the chef would write on the chalk board our daily tasks. When I saw lemon merengue, I thought wow, I had seen it in the bakers shops up north where I lived in Yorkshire, I had seen it in cook books, I had even tasted it before and I loved it, but now I was going to actually make it myself.

Lemon custards and puddings have been made since medieval times but the merengue itself wasn't perfected till the 17th century. Apparently, it was the Quakers who invented lemon custards in the 1700s, it was a pastry chef businesswoman in 1806 that expanded on the lemon custard and invented lemon merengue. Now lemon merengue as we know it today is a 19th century product and there are numerous ways to make it and I remember vividly that morning in the class room like it was yesterday and I was raring to go. As this spotty young kid that thought he knew it all we weighed our ingredients then the chef gave us a demo of what had to be done part of that was lining the flan case with sweet pastry and filling it with rice to blind bake it before we put the filling in. The chef left the class for half an hour and we cracked on. I decided to cook my base open without the rice grains so I could get the filling in quicker and impress the chef on my speed, but the oven temperature was too

46

hot and it burnt the base. Panic had set in and my class mates were taking the piss.

'Chef will be back soon,' said one of them, 'And you are in the shit Mick.'

He was right so I rushed over and made some more pastry rolled it out as quick as I could and lined the flan ring again, by now the others were pouring in the lemon mixture and making the merengue. I poured my lemon mix onto the raw pastry with a smile on my face, then I piped the merengue on. Surprised faces were looking on at me as the chef came back in.

'Well done all of you,' said chef, 'As soon as you are ready get them in the oven.'

We all put our lemon merengues in the oven and started to clean up I still had a smile on my face thinking I had got away with it, after about twenty minutes there was smoke coming from my oven.

'Collins your oven is on fire!' chef shouted running towards me.

'What the!' I exclaimed.

My class mates were in stitches laughing.

'Quiet you lot!' screamed the chef.

He opened the oven door as the black acrid smoke rose into the class room, from the flan ring was a big bubble which had pushed all the mixture over onto the bottom of the oven caramelising and cracking on the electric cooker element.

'You didn't blind bake that Collins you fucking idiot,' said Chef, 'And what flour did you use?'

I realised I had made a ball's up with the flour and had used self-raising instead of plain which had caused the pastry to rise in oven at the same time pushing all the filling out. It was very rare we used selfraising flour it was always plain which we added baking powder to if the recipe needed it, trust me to use the wrong flour, I got the bollocking of my life and it took me hours to scrub the oven clean.

Let's make the lemon merengue hopefully with more success than I did all them years ago.

*****

Using the sweet pastry recipe from the Apple pie recipe, grease a flan ring as shown above if you have a flan ring with a removeable bottom it would be an asset.

For the filling

Lemons x 4 juice and zest.

Cornflour two and a quarter oz.

Caster sugar 9oz.

Egg yolks x 6.

Water16 fluid oz.

*****

For the merengue.

Egg whites x 4.

Caster sugar 8oz.

Cornflour 2 x teaspoons full

*****

Put some greaseproof over the pastry tuck it in and fill with rice or dried peas cook for about 15 minutes at 180, once again keep your eye on it don't let it over brown.

Once you get a biscuit colour reduce the oven to 160 for about 10 minutes.

Mix the lemon zest and juice with the cornflour.

Bring the water to the boil add the lemon cornflour mixture and stir till it has thickened then remove from the heat.

In a bowl mix the sugar and egg yolks and carefully whisk into the lemon mixture in the pan stir over a medium heat till thickened, don't leave it. set aside for a few minutes then pour onto the cooked pastry case.

Whip the egg whites until soft peaks form slowly add the caster sugar whisking all the time (better with an electric whisk) add the cornflour and whisk again. Either pipe it on the lemon or just blob it on and swirl it, have a go at piping it is easier than what you think.

Now for the hard bit, pop it in the oven for 15 minutes at 160 to 170 the filling will set and the merengue should be a lightly golden beige crisp, I did mine in the halogen oven the results are in the photos above, leave to cool then put in the fridge. This is one of the tougher recipes to make in this book but it is a lovely dessert, I once made a bad mistake when I was a young trainee and I will never forget it. get all your ingredients and flan ring ready first then give it a go follow my instructions and you won't go far wrong.

Quiche Separabit

HOMEMADE FISH CAKES

     When out on exercise apart from Zero Hotel (the officers mess truck) where I had the luxury of two household gas cookers with calor gas, I always had the faithful number one burner shown on the left below and in my opinion one of the finest field burners going. There was another burner the number 5 cooker bottom left which was also fuelled with gas or petrol and one that I very rarely used plus there was always something going wrong with it. The main compo stove for the tank troops was the trusty hexamine cooker with the little white fire lighter blocks perfect size for their mess tins plus the hexamine blocks were perfect for lighting the barbeques on the squadron smokers. During the late 1970s and the beginning of the 1980s a new cooker burner came into service, the cooks' trailer, a modern cook set for a modern army was the slogan, this could be towed by a land rover or a Bedford. To the front of the trailer were four burners and at the rear were two large ovens. The whole thing was mainly fuelled with calor gas, the sides dropped down to expose working surfaces, pots and pans and serving equipment, six-gallon containers could still be used on these burners as you can see, but the boiling time of water for example was no match to the mighty number one burner. When I first saw these cook's trailer's I initially thought it would be a great asset to us cooks for field catering and with our knowledge of the compo we would be able to improve on our standards. Some people liked them for the convenience, they were cleaner and easier to light, but they were a pain in the arse to pack away and when we got back to camp they had to be stripped and cleaned to look like new, they were very rarely used on exercises in our regiment I think I worked on one twice and personally I thought they were a pile of shit, I much preferred the number one burner for its simplicity and speed. If you were in a wood with full camouflage you would always be able to find the cooks tent by the distinct

roaring sound of the number one burner.

Going back to the old army composite packs one of the menus used to have one with salmon in, this particular ten-man pack had two tins in the size of a normal soup tin, it was beautiful. Please let me stress that ten-man packs were never given to the tank crews, they would get the more convenient four-man pack so they could store it on their tanks and if my memory serves me correctly there was no salmon in these smaller packs either but I stand to be corrected. As I have said before we could do wonders with compo providing, we had flour, eggs and baking powder and other little things we needed. Now before leaving camp I would scout around and would try and get all the luxury items such as onions, carrots and other goodies that I needed to make the compo look and taste better, for me cooking in the field was where I seemed to shine in fact there were things I did in the field that I couldn't do in camp, like bread for instance, more on that later though.

Back to the tinned salmon we would open about ten tins drain them and remove the soft bones and skin, finally we would flake it into small pieces. Also, in these packs were mashed potato powder or POM as we called it, we would make a thick mash and add a load of cooked softened onions then the salmon and fold it all together with eggs to bind it. All that was required now was to fry them in the compo axle grease margarine, or if we had an oven, we could bake them, we would get about 70 or 80 fish cakes depending on the size and we served them for lunch in the field with parsley sauce which you can make from the bechamel sauce in this book.

*****

For four fishcakes.

Four medium potatoes peeled cooked and mashed.

One small tin of tuna or salmon, or fresh fish of your choice.

Prawns (save some for decoration)

One onion finely chopped and cooked.

Egg yolks 2 chopped chives or parsley.

Salt and pepper.

Lemon and tomato (optional) for garnish

Fresh bread crumbs 4 to 6 slices.

Egg wash.

Strain the cooked potatoes and make sure they are dry sometimes it is better to put them in the microwave to cook then cut them in half and scoop them out.

Once the potato is mashed add the finely chopped cooked onion, tuna, prawns, salt and pepper, egg yolks, chives and a few handfuls of breadcrumbs, mix it all together if it is a bit sticky add more breadcrumbs till you can mould it, leave to cool in fridge.

Cut into four and make into balls as shown, egg and bread them then when they are covered press them slightly to the cake shape, place on a greased tray and back in the fridge again till you are ready to cook them. 140 to 160 in the oven, as with all my recipes keep your eye on them all ovens are different, if you prefer just fry them till golden on each side. Plate up and if you want to be cheffy garnish as above serve with parsley sauce. They are lovely when served hot with mashed potatoes, garden peas and loads of parsley sauce,

TANKIES EGG BANJO

On a lighter note this is my little tribute to the 4th/7th Royal Dragoon Guards who I am certain if you are reading this you will recognise this tasty treat, and maybe it will bring a smile of remembrance to their faces, and for my civilian friends you are about to learn how to cook the tankies favourite food. Over my 22 years' service I did countless exercises as a cook and an SQMS (Squadron Quartermaster Sergeant) storeman. Whenever we stopped to replenish the tank crews, we would see something that the health and safety today would string us up by the testicles for. Oiled up greasy, dust ridden, covered in diesel and smoke fumes and I am not on about the tanks I am talking about the crew themselves; it was a sight to behold as they were laughing and joking, smoking and drinking beer. One particular crewman normally the driver who was greasier and oiled up more than the rest of them put together would be cooking fried eggs at the side of the tank on a little hexamine cooker and handing these delights up to his crew mates, hand prints would adorn these tankies delicacy's as his mates would grab them putting more dirty prints onto the once white bread till eventually it got to the bloke that was going to eat it, they would devour these treats and think nothing of the grease, oil and dirt. As long as these fellows got their eggs and bread on the SQMSs replens, they were happy.

I had seen it so many times over the years it didn't bother me, but even to this day it makes me smile when I think about it, happy days.

*****

For two people.

Four slices of bread.

Butter or (cheap margarine).

Two eggs

A spoonful of marmite and a pastry brush.

*****

Butter the bread, fry the egg and flip over, put on the bread and put the top slice on, cut in half. hehe

Finally, put the marmite in a dish with a very small droplet of water, mix together with the pastry brush it still needs to be sticky, then paint it onto the palm of your hand and fingers, place your hand on the egg banjo and press take your hand away and hey presto you have a tankies egg banjo with greasy hand print, but seriously it tastes delicious because I ate this one.

BECHAMEL SAUCE

I make a lot of Bechamel these days for me it's just a posh word for a silky white sauce but I suppose it sounds good. For those of you that see my grub on facebook you will notice that I use it a lot for my cooking especially cheese sauce, but you can add parsley for the fish sauce, or you could use the thickened version for supreme sauce. For this particular sauce in the past I have had loads of bollockings for doing it the cowboy way which is to use cornflour which cuts the time down by half. No matter what we did we couldn't hide the fact from the master chef that we had used cornflour, he could see straight away without even tasting it, the cowboy sauce would give off a shiny sheen and once the chef saw this we were in the shit. I tried to make it by whisking flour and water together then add it to the milk but it didn't work it was full of little lumps, the amount of extra duty's I got for cheating this sauce I have lost count. The thing was it was harder to find a cowboy method that I could get away with rather than doing it properly but it was fun trying. I suppose at the time we thought we might just get away with it, maybe just the once but we never did.

It was very rare that a cook was locked up in guardroom in my regiment, although I was in once or twice in the early 1970s. On exercise Seedy Simpson told us the continuing story of Gopper Price the unhygienic cook he used to work with when they were with the Boneheads who was always trying to work his ticket, this time he had been AWOL (Absent without official leave). Anyway, Gopper had been caught and brought back to Germany and locked up in the guardroom until his court martial date. Nobody knew how, but one evening he went to the toilet in the nick and managed to pull the bars off the window, he escaped to the main square and broke into a car putting a coat on that he found on the back seat then he hotwired the car. Never one for luck Gopper drove to the guardroom and the fucking car broke down at the barrier, the guard commander saw what had happened and called the guard out to give Gopper a push to start the car out of the main gate, on the way out he even asked the barrier guard for a cig before driving off into the night. Gopper was caught six months later and when he was brought back to camp the poor guard commander was still doing his extras.

Bechamel to make a pint.

*****

Butter 2oz.

Plain flour 2oz

Milk one pint.

Salt and white pepper

Melt the butter in the sauce pan and add the flour to make a roux, slowly add the milk till you get the consistency you need sometimes I like it thicker especially if I make lasagnes and such like. Once this is done let it simmer for a minute to cook the flour out but keep stirring, pour a drop of double cream in if you want. Add parsley or cheese or whatever you are using it for, in the one above I have put cheese in.

If you do want to make it the cowboy way then go ahead it still does the job, just put a pint of milk in a saucepan on the stove mix a few tablespoons of cornflour with some of the milk, when it starts to boil whisk in the cornflour mix, add salt and pepper, then get on your horse and ride out of town. You can buy the sauce in a packet if you want but I have found that after all the extras I got all them years ago it is easier to do it the proper way plus it tastes better.

PORK GROWLERS

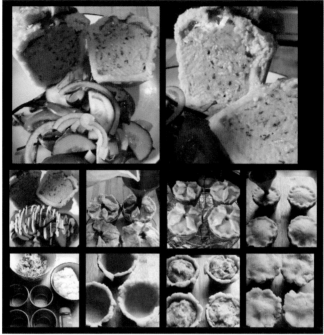

(Homemade pork pies)

Originally these were not on my favourite list but a few months ago an old friend of mine asked me if I would make them and I agreed. I will be honest I haven't made this type of pie since I went back to the catering school in the late 70s on an upgrading course. I actually really enjoyed making them and it brought back a lot of memories from my course days. I can remember trying to make a pie on exercise without an oven, well sort of, it was an idea that I had thought about but I had never tested it, Seedy Simpson said it was a shit idea and it wouldn't work, but I was going to try and prove him wrong.

When I was a kid my dad used to use a blow torch to burn the paint off doors before painting them, he would fill it with fuel and pump it up to get the pressure then light it. The number one burner field cooker is best described as a big blow torch it worked in a similar way to the little torch my dad used all them years ago, only a hell of a lot bigger and fuelled with petrol. Once these things were blasting, they could boil a six-gallon container of water in about twenty minutes and they had the sound of a jet engines afterburner. Once we got to a location, we could unload these burners and light them and within 25 minutes there would be an urn of tea ready for the troops. The normal practice was to dig the burner into a trench for better heat efficiency, but we never did this unless we had a keen cook sergeant or corporal with us, so we would set the burner and stands up on the flat ground fill it with petrol and then pump it up to about 40lb psi all this was dangerously done in the same area. For safety reasons we were supposed to use a filling area 30 feet away, then a lighting area 30 feet away, then once the burner was lit there was a handle so we could carry it back to the trench and yes it was lit! bollocks to that though, it was much more dangerous, easier and lazier to do it all in the cooking area, had the health and safety been about in those days we would have had our balls on a plate. These burners had been known to blow up but I never saw one explode in all the years I used them, there was a safety feature on top of the fuel tank which was called a safety nipple as that is what it looked like, a nipple, if the pressure got too high this nipple was the weakest point of the tank and would fly out releasing the air from the tank, I never ever saw this happen but I can imagine the escape of the pressurised air combined with the petrol fumes from the main tank would have spoiled someone's day, I was told if you were ever stood over the burner when this happened the nipple would blast out with the velocity of a rifle bullet hitting you in the head and killing you instantly and if that didn't get you the blast from the spray of petrol would burn you alive and if you were lucky enough to survive all that you would get the bollocking of your life from the master chef for not adhering to the safety protocol.

Anyway back in the burner trench and in front of the flame would be one or two burner stands each one had three holes for the cooking pots the hottest one nearest the burner and obviously the hole furthest away would be the coolest, so how do I make a pie with a number one burner and no oven? I thought. On the furthest away hole on the stand I put one of the spare end plates across to block it, the burner end plates normally go at the back of the stands to keep the heat in. I got the idea for this concoction from putting baked potatoes in tinfoil and cooking them in the fire like we used to do on bonfire night when we were kids, I rolled out sections of pastry filled the centre with compo stewed steak and rolled it up similar to a poor man's beef wellington. These pastry pies when rolled would be about 18 inches long and looked like a jam roly poly. I would then put it on tinfoil which was well greased with plenty of the axle grease compo margarine, then it went on a 20x10x2 tray on the back-burner end plate, I remember just doing two as I wasn't sure of the outcome. Once all the other burner holes were covered with other containers they would get more heat, it would take a while but you could see the foil expanding, it was too risky to turn them over in case I split the foil, so I covered them with another 20x10x2 in effect making a type of oven. Of course it was all guesswork and trial and error, once I thought they were cooked I took them of, Seedy would be taking the piss as I started to unwrap them, the foil took a bit of removing but they turned out sort of okay they reminded me of suet puddings, when I turned them over I could see the underneath that had been touching the burner plate was slightly browned, I decided to portion them as best I could. The troops ate them but it would have been easier to make a pot of stew and dumplings or a pie, but that's what we did, sometimes the ideas worked and sometimes they didn't that is what made field cooking so much fun, unfortunately this one didn't work and it wasn't my finest hour.

Hot water paste is very easy to make and it is very pliable it's a bit like kids play dough, best to use it while it is still warm as it is easier to mould and shape, and I hardly needed any flour for dusting the board. For these four pies I used the mix below if you need to make more just double it up.

Hot water paste.

*****

Plain flour 12oz.

Lard 3oz.

Water 6 ¾ fluid oz.

Salt.

*****

This is dead simple, add salt to the flour.

In a saucepan bring the water and lard to the boil so it melts.

Once it as melted add the flour and salt to the pan and mix well with a wooden spoon, it will all come together, put it in a dish with a cloth over and leave for 20 minutes while you prepare the filling.

Growler is a Yorkshire thing for pork pies although in the past I have heard of a NAAFI growler, if I went into a pie shop down south and asked for a growler in my Yorkshire accent they wouldn't have a clue, if it was a woman in the shop she would probably think I was a pervert "Can I have a warm growler love?" The filling is so simple and for these four pies I got about a 1lb of lean pork mince or 500g it was about £1.99 in Lidl.

The filling.

*****

Minced pork 1lb or 500g.

Salt and black pepper

Tablespoon of sage.

And that's it, in a bowl mix it all together with your hand till everything is combined, it does look a lot but you need plenty.

Grease the moulds and get the warm pastry and cut it into four then cut a quarter of each piece for the top, roll each piece out and put it on the mould use your fingers to mould it into the sides, make sure the pastry comes over the top of the mould as it is important for the lid to stick to this, any cracks or little holes repair them with the surplus pastry otherwise the juices from the meat will escape. Divide the meat into four and press into each pie it is better if it is full to the top as it will shrink when cooking, push the bottom end of a wooden spoon into each pie it makes a decent hole for letting the steam out and putting the gel in later, I used a little funnel as I will use this to fill the pie with jelly later. Egg wash the pies and decorate with leaves if you want, egg wash again then I cooked these in the halogen oven I cooked them for about 2 hrs 15 minutes, at 120. Keep looking at them, the beauty of the halogen oven is I can watch them all the time, after about an hour I egg washed them again and I turned the oven down to 110 for the remaining time. When they are cooked leave them to cool. I used a Dr Oetkers vege gel with a vege stock cube one sachet makes a pint and I added the cube I made it with half a pint of water to be sure it set and it was fine but you have to be quick and follow the instructions, of course you can use gelatine, you need to fill them while they are still luke warm and still in the moulds then when they are fully cool get them back in the fridge overnight if possible. Serve with a nice salad or if you are like me serve them hot covered with loads of mushy peas and mint sauce. I was very pleased with my attempt at these little pies and I am considering making a large one for Christmas in a loaf tin.

ALICES BREXIT COTTAGE PIE

     This cottage pie is made with turkey mince, me and Mandy are not big meat eaters and our main choice is chicken or turkey. However, you can use beef, lamb or whatever you want. We prefer turkey as it is lighter in fat value, this cottage pie you have probably seen numerous times on facebook when I make it for the kids it is quick and easy to make, I normally make it the night before. I like to pre-cook the meat base and put it in the dish in the fridge so it sets, I tend to make it a bit thicker, best to do it like this because if it is too thin the mash will push it out of the dish. When we made these with the compo rations in the field, we would mash the stewed steak and put it in the 20x10x2 inch serving trays normally we would make the POM or mashed potato and put this on top followed by the good old compo grated processed cheese. Compo cheese was not to everyone's taste, I personally loved it, but a lot of the troops would leave it, when we got back to camp the SQMS would collect the surplus compo from the tanks and there would be a lot of this tinned cheese which would be sent to the cookhouse. So, if it went in a sandwich a lot of the lads wouldn't be very happy as I will explain in a minute.

     Sometimes when we were on exercise especially the annual firing for the chieftains buses would be laid on to take some of the troops back to barracks, now when I say buses I don't mean luxury coaches with reclining seats, head rests and ventilation, they were just white boneshaking cattle truck buses with the old fashioned hard seats, if you were tired it was impossible to get any sleep and if you wanted a piss you would have to use a coke bottle that was passed around and emptied out of the window. The driver would normally be a German civilian whose gear changing skills would rattle your bones and if you were lucky enough to nod off, you would soon be awakened as he would hit every fucking bump in the road. The SSM would normally sit near the front to keep the restless troops under control, there were sixty bored squaddies on each of these buses just wanting to get back to barracks so they could get showered and cleaned up. I remember Seedy on one of these buses once and we were traveling from exercise back to our barracks, all of a sudden, a shout rang out.

'COR! Eyes right lads,' shouted Seedy, 'Get a load of the top bollocks on that.'

Everyone would pile over to the right of the bus to get a glimpse of Seedy's sighting, the bus would rock to the right swerving on the road from the weight of the rush of bodies wanting to get a look at the first bird they had seen in weeks only to find it was a woman about sixty with tits down to her knee caps.

Seedy would be sat laughing at their reaction.

'Behave yourself Simpson!' said the SSM.

The lads would sit back down muttering, 'You bastard Seedy.'

After a while the SSM would have a couple of blokes walking through the bus issuing the packed lunches from cardboard boxes, these were better known as horror bags and as they were passed out you could hear the moans and groans from the troops.

'Oh, fucking hell.' Came the shouts, 'What delights have we got today? Hope it's not gonna be that minging cheese possessed.'

These horror bags were so bad that even the cooks would moan about them and we fucking made them. The brown paper bags would normally have a couple of sandwiches which were compo processed cheese and luncheon meat with the horrible axle grease margarine spread on the hard-stale bread which was days old, there would be a bruised apple or soft orange, one of those little packets of biscuits with three custard creams, a drink and a two fingered Kit Kat. The drink, Kit Kat and biscuits were the first things to go probably because the cooks had never touched them, maybe they would have a couple of bites from the apple and the rest would go in the bin. This was the time when us cooks would get the worst grief from the lads.

'The fitters and turners have struck again,' someone shouted.

'Why do you call us that?' said Lefty Wright scratching his head.

'Because you fit it into pots and turn it into shit.' Came the reply.'

Everyone was laughing including the SSM, this is the type of stick we got all the time but we just tried to let it go over our shoulders. Apart from the horror bags I thought that under the circumstances and overall, we did a good job and deep down the lads knew this. Once the troops were in a confined environment like this bus it was a recipe for verbal horseplay and we could give as much as we took. Right let's get back to cooking the cottage pie.

For two to four people.

*****

Two onions finely chopped.

One large carrot chopped.

Turkey, beef or lamb mince packs from the supermarket.

Potatoes 2lb.

Butter for potatoes.

Bisto granules.

Grated cheese of your choice.

Water.

Put the onion, carrots and the mince in a saucepan with some oil and seal off season with salt and pepper.

Once it has sealed cover with water and bring to the boil then simmer and let it reduce so there is just a small amount of liquid but you don't want it dry, thicken with the Bisto granules you won't need a lot, it needs to be nice and thick so it sets but not too thick, let it cool then fridge it for an hour. Put the potatoes on to cook, mash them with some butter and put the top layer on the mince followed by the cheese. All that needs doing now is a hot oven about 180 to till golden brown. You may think I am telling you how to suck eggs making cottage, because everyone makes cottage pie, but this is a quick and simple way to make it, if you are worried about Brexit this is a nice cheap recipe hehe, or if you have a hectic life style or need something quick on the table then this is it. It is a bit of a cowboy recipe I know, but you can make it the proper way by adding the flour to the meat and roux style followed by tomato puree it is entirely your choice. Seedy Simpson was an expert on sex and cowboy methods and one day when he was hungover in the larder department he cooked a load of mince for the cottage pies he put a tin of tomato paste in the meat and hoping to fool the master chef he thickened it with a batter mix of plain flour and water to save making the roux, when it cooled it was still too thin and you could see the white flour lumps floating on top, Seedy give it a good whisking hoping to remove the offending lumps hoping it would thicken up when it cooled then he put the trays in the freezer. After a few hours they were solid and Seedy put the mash on which was no problem till the next day when they were put in the oven to brown the potato sunk down pushing the gravy like mince and white blobs of flour all over the bottom of the oven. I can tell you the master chef was none too pleased and Seedy got quite a few duty cooks, plus he spent quite a few hours cleaning the oven. Seedy was a married man and said it was a good excuse for not going home to his wife so when he finished each of his extras, he would go straight on the piss in the squadron bar then end up in a dance bar somewhere in town with some hippocrocodillapig. Sometimes he wouldn't even go home and stay out all night with his conquests, knowing he had to be back at work at 8am the next day for is next extra, I never met Seedy's wife but I honestly felt sorry for her, Seedy may have been married but he lived the life of a single soldier.

EGG CUSTARDS

This egg custard story always reminds me of a certain slot machine when I was stationed in Tidworth in the early 70s. We used to make hundreds of these custards, fortunately we had a hand machine where we could put the sweet pastry in the mould and by pulling a lever it would squash them into shape including the crimped edges. We would put them on big black baking trays which would hold about 50, once we had put the egg custard mixture in the pastry shells, we would open the oven door and then carefully try and get the full tray in the oven without any of the egg custard spilling onto the tray, I can see me now picking the tray up and very slowly making my way to the oven, my tongue outside the side of my mouth in concentration, to make it harder my fellow cooks would be taking the piss and trying to make me laugh the bastards. Of course, there was an easy way to do this which sometimes just stares you in the face but you can't see it. The answer is to put the tray in the oven first then with a jug fill the lined moulds with the custard while you are stood at the oven then sprinkle with nutmeg, all you have to do then is slide the tray into the oven and shut the door. A very good cook friend of mine, his name was Lefty Wright who thought he could do them quicker and better, he was only a young lad fresh from the catering school who thought he knew more than the master chef, I remember he got about ten extra duty cooks, now the duty cook would normally start about lunch time then he would work through till about 9pm in the evening, it would include serving late meals, veg and preparation for the following day, making the dreaded brown sauce (Gravy), the guard room box and cleaning. If you were given extra duty cooks you would start at 8.30 in the morning and work through and believe me it was a long slog because I had my share, most of the time you would get them all in one lump so Lefty as you can imagine was knackered after ten days. Anyway, what Lefty did to get them was he decided to cook the pastry bases blind, once they were cooked and cooled, he came up with this concoction of boiling milk with sugar and yellow colouring, vanilla essence and thicken it all with cornflour. He then poured this mixture into the cooked pastry cases, sprinkled them with nutmeg and put them in the fridge and I have to say they did look like egg custards hehe. A few hours later he took them out of the fridge to get them out of the moulds for traying up, normally you would do this by grabbing the mould and giving it a quick shake and it would drop out, a normal egg custard will stick to the pastry as the tart comes out of the mould, but it was just the inside of Lefty's concoction that came out, it was a wobbling jelly of milky yellow goo. He tried to get the pastry out of the moulds in one piece hoping he could save the day by just dropping the wobbly goo back in and that no one would notice, chef did.

'Sorry chef the custard is a bit slack in the moulds,' whimpered Lefty.

'It's you that's fucking slack Wright!' screamed the master chef,' Slack as a bag of fucking knackers, take ten!'

This was one of the most blatant cowboy methods I have ever seen, Lefty was given his ten extras and I would shake his hand and congratulate him, there was method in our madness. So, where does the slot machine come in, I hear you say? As young lads we were always short of money we would get paid at the beginning of the month and two days later we would be skint, so sometimes doing duty cook was a bonus and we would put ourselves in the firing line to get extras it was like a competition but we had our reasons. In the dining room was a Tic Tac Toe bandit it wasn't a one-armed type but the new electronic ones, the dining room had been broken into on a few occasions but the would-be thieves never got anything from the machine plus it would have been risky with the guard wondering around the camp. Anyway, for security, it became the duty cooks job to wheel the machine through the kitchen into the rest room to keep it locked up and out of view of would be thieves. However, it wasn't the duty cooks job to turn it upside down and shake the machine, when we turned it up right again we could hear the money dropping down to the bottom of the bandit we then stuck two 12 inch knifes in the trap door at the bottom tilted it and the money slid out onto the floor. The next day when the machine was wheeled back to the dining room and switched on it would be flashing and beeping like hell. Had we been caught we would have been jailed for sure, me and Lefty were on to a good thing and easy money so we started to do silly things to get extras so we could get on duty cook to rob it, I remember when Lefty threw an egg at the kitchen extractor knowing the chef was watching him, he got two extras, when the chef went into his office Lefty turned around to me with thumbs up and winked. I once lit a fag up at the hotplate and the master chef bollocked me and gave me three extras, secretly we were happy as me and Lefty knew that by doing this we could get at the machine when we were short of money. We did it a quite few times and eventually the bandit was taken away because the firm that owned it said it wasn't making any money. Ironically a few days before Lefty had dropped the jackpot but hardly any cash was paid out so he complained to the machine man when he came to take it away demanding he be paid his winnings hehe. Me and Lefty were disappointed when it was taken but we had quite a few good nights out on the beer from it. From then on, our extra duty competition stopped to the dismay of the rest of the cooks because now they would have to start doing their own duty's.

Simple to make. You can either do them in individual moulds or a flan ring if you prefer, I made mine in a muffin tin. If like me you make them in a muffin tin let them cool then put a tray over them and turn the whole thing upside down to get them out, they should all drop down on the tray, simply turn them over and plate up as shown in my photo.

Egg custards.

*****

Sweet paste recipe from the apple pie.

Milk one pint.

Eggs four

Caster sugar 5 tablespoons.

Vanilla essence.

Nutmeg.

*****

Line the moulds with the sweet pastry make sure that there are no air bubbles if there are use a cocktail stick, press the pastry in the moulds then trim off.

Add the eggs, caster sugar and vanilla essence to the milk and whisk, strain into another jug then fill the pastry cases with the custard sprinkle with nutmeg and cook slowly for about 30 minutes at 130, as in all my cooking keep your eye on them.

HOMEMADE GYROS AND RICE

I loved German food and even after all these years I miss the bratwurst, currywurst, chips with mayonnaise, schnitzels I could go on. Gyros is Greek but they used to cook it in the German imbiss or takeaway, it was beautiful and since I left Germany, I have only ever tasted a good one when we were on holiday in Majorca about 16 years ago. You can buy them in Iceland or Lidl but they don't taste the same. In Detmold there was one place and it was called fat Sam's and it was the best gyros I have ever tasted in my life. I used to get two sometimes and what I didn't eat I would have it cold for my breakfast, the thing I like the most apart from the lovely flavoured meat which was turning on the spit was the tomato rice it was so simple yet delicious and it was a perfect accompaniment to the gyros with the lovely sliced red onions and salad, I could eat one now. You can buy a small spit if you have hundreds of pounds to waste, then you are still not forced to get the same taste, I have seen loads of different recipes for gyros and I have tried different ways myself even in the slow cooker. For this I sliced the belly pork up into strips and sealed it off in the frying pan with garlic and spices, then I put it in the slow cooker for about five hours, the pork tasted lovely with the tomato rice but not a patch on fat Sam's. Now I will put my neck on the line because this recipe is the nearest and best I have got to the gyros that I remember from Detmold, unless you

69

already have your spices, you will need a few, I went on amazon and ordered a packet of Souvlaki Gyros mix they were £2.50 with free delivery and I got them the next day, I liked this because they are already mixed in the correct quantity's so there is no guessing

If you want to give it a go here it is.

For two people.

*****

Four pork steaks 500 g cut into strips.

One onion chopped.

Button mushrooms

Salt.

Black pepper.

Souvlaki Gyros mix I used four tablespoons full

Garlic one whole bulb.

*****

Patna rice one cup and two cups of water.

Tomato puree.

Oil and best butter

Finely chopped onions and mushrooms for the rice, cooked in the microwave for three minutes.

*****

Put the rice and water in a microwavable bowl, cling film and microwave for four minutes. Take the cling film off and stir, re cling film again and cook for a further four minutes leave it covered till it cools down a bit as the rice will still be cooking, or buy a packet of uncle Bens Patna rice.

Trim the pork and cut into strips as shown, put in a container with the gyros mix, mix thoroughly then cover with cling film and put in the fridge, overnight if you can.

Mix the tomato puree, cooked onion and mushrooms with the rice and check the seasoning, if you want to save time then use the uncle bens packet rice from the supermarket. Put all the rice into two microwave timbale or ramakin dish and cover ready for heating.

Put the oil and butter in a thick frying pan and melt, add the meat onions, garlic and mushrooms and cook steadily till you get a nice colour, don't be tempted to stir it all the time just leave it for a few minutes to brown slightly. In the meantime, heat the rice in the microwave and turn it out on the plate, I have made mine look fancy by putting the onion slices over the meat and serve it with salad. Fat Sam would have served chips and mayonnaise with it.

That is the best and as near as I can get without a spit, still not as good as fat Sam's in Detmold, but as near as damn it. If you look closely at the label in the photo you can see the spices are oregano, paprika, salt, pepper and cumin, but you will have to guess them, if you have these spices I wouldn't overdo them, at first maybe put quarter of a teaspoon of each spice but be careful with the cumin, pepper and paprika, if you like it then fair enough put it in. With gyros I find I am experimenting all the time so as I said this recipe is the best and the taste is superb, good luck.

71

LASAGNE

This is one I make quite often for the kids, you can make it the day before and it is easy, gone are the days when we used to have to cook the pasta sheets in salt water which made it a more time consuming job, now we just by a packet of them ready to cook sheets and layer them into the meat and cheese. Believe it or not this could be made with compo, well in a fashion I suppose. Always looking to do something different on exercise we would sit around the number one burner on an evening in a freezing German wood having a beer or six and a smoke and we would chat about our ideas, it was my old friend Lefty Wright who came up with this one. I remember this exercise particularly well because Lefty wanted to go for a number two, or a shovel recce as we squaddies called it. being with a tank regiment we wore green coveralls like a boiler suit so when you took them off you undid the clasps at the front and you would peel them off your shoulders then take them off like normal trousers, I think you get the picture. Lefty grabbed the shovel, bog roll and a torch and off he went.

Once you found a decent spot you would dig your hole then remove your coveralls, you would peel them off your shoulders and make sure they were round your ankles before you squat down to do your business. Lefty didn't do this properly and when he squatted, he was so desperate he did it in back of his coveralls, he was totally oblivious to this until he wiped his arse and pulled the coveralls up over his shoulders. Three days of warm compo poo was stuck to his back complete with bog paper, we heard the scream from the cook's tent.

'Oh, fuck no!' screamed Lefty.

We all ran to where he was because we thought at first something had happened to him, when we got there, he had pulled his coveralls off again, he looked a sight caked in shit as we stood there and shone our torches on him, once we realised what he had done we started pissing ourselves laughing. He was plastered in poo and the bloody stench I can smell even now. We told him the best thing to do was to strip off which he did so he could get cleaned up, he ended up burying the coveralls in the hole he had dug for his shovel recce, at least he saved on the bog roll. Perhaps this is not a story for a cook book but Lefty had us in stitches. On the subject of bog roll there was some in the compo packs it was like greaseproof paper it reminded me of the stuff my mother used to get when we were kids, it was called IZAL, do you remember it? In the ten-man compo pack there was a small packet with about ten pieces of this paper, so that was one piece of shiny paper for each man thank god we didn't all get the shits at the same time hehe. Most of us brought our own soft rolls from the NAAFI before the exercise started it was a very important part of our exercise kit, we used to call it comfy bum for obvious reasons.

Anyway sorry about that and back to the cooking and we were sat around the number one burner talking compo ideas, Lefty said what about lasagne? which was quite feasible with compo, we would mash the stewed steak with garlic and tomatoes and herbs, cheese sauce wasn't a problem but lasagne pasta sheets were the sticking point. Lefty came up with the idea of pancakes we had the flour, dried milk, water and eggs, it was so simple and I never thought of using pancakes so the next day we tried it out, lefty cooked the pancakes and we layered it with the mashed stewed steak, tomato and garlic and topping it with a cheese possessed sauce and it worked, the lads loved it. I have made this on numerous occasions for the family with pasta sheets and pancakes and I have to say the pancake version is delicious, try it!

Here is my recipe for both versions for about four people.

*****

Minced beef, turkey, Quorn, chicken, lamb whatever you fancy 500g.

One whole onion chopped.

Button mushrooms quartered.

One whole garlic bulb crushed.

One small jar of pasta sauce.

Cheese sauce from my bechamel recipe.

Tablespoon of Bisto granules (optional)

Pasta lasagne sheets.

(If you want to try pancakes instead of pasta use my pancake recipe from cheese and onion pancakes you will need about four)

*****

Cook the meat, onion, mushrooms and garlic in a saucepan with a drop of oil, my preference is turkey mince. As you seal it some juices will form you need to boil them out till the meat becomes dry then you add the pasta sauce, bring back to the boil and simmer for a few minutes. It needs to be a thick consistency, put the Bisto into to ensure a thicker sauce as shown, put it to one side and let it cool while you make the cheese sauce.

Once the meat as cooled put a thin layer in the dish followed by the pasta, then another thin layer of meat followed by the pasta. I like at least four layers, if you are using pancakes exactly the same just substitute it for the pasta, finally pour the nice thick cheese sauce over the top and sprinkle with a bit more grated cheese, cook in the oven at 140 for about 45 minutes. I love this recipe because when you cut the lasagne it portions perfectly, you get a nice chunk on your plate, some people tend to make the sauce too runny which results with the lasagne spreading all over the plate if you know what I mean. Anyway, give it a go but do try it with pancakes.

HOMEMADE CHEESE CAKE

     To make this I purchased some tinfoil bases as most of the things I cook in this book go to friends and family. The first time I saw this made with cream cheese was in Cyprus in 1988 30 years ago I was the regimental ration store man there for six months in Nicosia. Apart from a rear party back in Detmold the whole regiment went to Cyprus it was one of the best times of my life with the regiment, I went on the advance party in early May 88 and returned to a chilly Detmold in November six months later and after the Cyprus sun it was a bit of a shock to the system. There was a cook sergeant his name was Bill and he must have been one of the oldest cooks in the ACC at the time, anyway he was a sound bloke and he had about six months left to go before his demob and retirement and he didn't give a shit. I gave him this huge container of cream cheese wondering if he could use it for anything, the next thing I knew there were these cheese cakes on the sweet counter for evening meal, I had a piece and it tasted gorgeous so much better than the packet rubbish, Bill told me the recipe and it was so easy and there was no cooking involved. At the time I had transferred from the ACC to the regiment but I still got on well with the cooks, Bill came up to me a few days later when I went for lunch.

     'Alice,' he said, 'The cooks have a darts match in Dhekelia on Friday night.'

Dhekelia was the main military base for our regiment it was about an hour's drive away.

'What's that got to do with me?' I said.

'Me and all the cooks want to go, and we are leaving about 2pm on Friday, so we wondered if you would finish up and serve the evening meal for us, it will be prepared for you and you can try your hand out at those cheese cakes.'

The cooks were stood behind the hotplate in anticipation.

I felt quite nervous as I hadn't done bulk catering for almost three years and that's a long time, I have to admit I was a bit nervous at the thought of it, isn't it funny? I had been doing catering for all those years and now I felt like a quivering wreck, I was going to be feeding about 70 to 80 for the evening meal I could feel the adrenalin pumping for what I was going to let myself in for.

'Okay Bill I will do it,' I said.

Cheers erupted from behind the hotplate as the cooks jumped for joy knowing they were all going on the piss.

I wasn't to be alone my counterpart in the ration stores would be there to assist me, a big Geordie lad, daft as a brush but he had a heart of gold. Once the cooks had gone, I was alone, but surprisingly I picked it up again very quickly, you never forget or so they say. As Bill said most of the meal was prepared and it was just a matter of serving it all up.

Friday came and I waved the excited cooks off, it was an enjoyable time feeding the troops again and it brought back some great cooking memories, plus I got the chance to make this delicious cheese cake.

For eight portions I made the two above.

*****

Crushed Shortbread or digestive biscuits 6oz.

Three table spoons of melted butter.

Cream Philadelphia cheese 200g.

Caster sugar 5 table spoons.

Juice of two lemons, grate the zest for the top.

Whipped cream 4 fluid oz

You will also need whipped cream for decoration as much as you like.

Strawberry's for decoration.

*****

Add the butter to the biscuit crumbs and mix together, press the biscuit mix into the cake tin put in the fridge. I put a round of greaseproof paper in the tins to make it easier to remove the cake when it was finished.

Mix the cream cheese, caster sugar and lemon juice together thoroughly, fold in the whipped cream and put the mixture onto the biscuit base, put in the fridge for a few hours or overnight.

I just decorated with swirls of whipped cream and strawberry's, then sprinkled some lemon zest over the top. There you have it, easy and no cooking.

ALICE'S QUICK STICKY TOFFEE PUDDING

     Back to the compo again I cannot remember which pack it was but there was a ginger pudding and it was delicious, it was sticky and had a Yorkshire parkin consistency but paler in colour, we used to just boil these in the tins like my mother used to do with the old Heinz treacle sponge. When it was time to serve up we would open the tins on the rotary can opener the steam would gush out as we punctured the hot cans they were served with the compo custard which we made with boiling water and loads of dried milk, if we didn't have custard powder we would thicken the milk with cornflour and add a touch of yellow colouring, when we were out on exercise this was lush. The only compo pudding better than this was the creamed rice pudding, it always reminded me of the ambrosia stuff my mother used to buy, I could eat it cold straight out of the tin and most of the tank crews used to love it. The ginger sponge was also very nice cold we used to open both ends of the tin and push it out, then slice it for cake for lunch time. My old friend Seedy Simpson was a dab hand with bread and butter puddings when we were on exercise, there was always plenty of bread and he would lace it with the compo marge and jam and make the egg custard with the powdered milk and put it in the oven, it was good stodgy hot pudding perfect for filling the troops on those cold winter days. I remember once Seedy sliced the ginger pudding and rich cake thinly and laid it out in a baking tray covering it with egg custard and put it in the field oven, it was superb like a rich man's bread and butter pudding, the lads went mad over it. Seedy was always a man for new ideas especially on the subject of sex where he would crease us up.

I found the recipe below a few years ago when I was working, if like me you like sticky toffee pudding then this an easy version you can either cook in in the microwave or if you prefer you can do it in the oven. It is dead easy to throw together and here is how to do it.

For four people.

*****

SR flour 6oz.

Eggs 2.

Butter 4oz.

Brown sugar 4oz. I used brown and white.

Dates 10 chopped and soak them in boiling water for ten minutes, drain and dry with kitchen roll.

Whipped cream or ice cream or both, custard if you like.

*****

Toffee sauce.

Butter 2oz.

Brown sugar 1oz.

Two tablespoons of double cream.

*****

You can look on the internet for numerous ways to do this pudding but for me this is the best and it is so simple to make.

Whisk the butter and sugar together in a bowl till it is smooth, add the eggs and flour, once again give it a good mix, fold in the dates.

Grease your little pudding moulds be they for the oven or the microwave and spoon the mixture in. That's it!

Oven cook at about 150 to 160 for 20 minutes if you think they are browning too quick turn the oven down slightly, keep your eye on them they should be firm to touch when cooked. Or the simple way is to microwave them on high for 2 minutes, if I was microwaving them, I would probably put some cling film over the mould. Leave to stand for two minutes before you turn them out.

To cook the toffee sauce. Put the butter, brown sugar and cream in a microwaveable jug and cook for one minute on high, take it out and stir then back in for a further 30 seconds, turn your puddings out and drizzle the sauce over them, serve with whipped cream or ice cream or if you are like me both of them. People will compliment you on these when they have tasted them, I used to get people saying to me "Why can't I get them as nice as that?" I used to think shall I tell them and let them know or shall I keep the simplicity of the recipe to myself, I did the latter hehe.

SCONE DOUGH PIZZA

Before I go into this recipe it's time to explain a bit more about the army composite rations which as I have said before were very versatile and with a bit of thought and of course flour we could do almost anything with it. These ten-man packs consisted of breakfast, lunch and dinner, also there were, jams, cheese, puddings, margarine (axle grease) sweets and chocolate, matches, coffee, tea sugar, powdered milk, salt, there was even toilet paper and a handy little blue container of salt. This pack was for ten men for one day and was used mainly for the rear echelons, if the cooks were in the field these were the packs we would use, as I said earlier the tank troops would have their own four-man packs as they fed themselves.

Breakfast would consist of beans, sausage and bacon grill, eggs and bread were issued by the SQMS Squadron quartermaster sergeant). Lunch would consist of packet soups, luncheon meat, salmon, pilchards, (yuck) cheese, oatmeal blocks and rich cake. Dinner was an assortment of corned beef, stewed steak, chicken supreme, steak and kidney puddings, goulash, chicken in brown sauce, the vegetables were peas, mixed veg and carrots depending on the pack. Assorted puddings, rice, apple, ginger, mixed fruit.

For us cooks lunch was always the meal where we would shine and use our inventiveness and imagination, now if we were lucky enough to get hold of tomatoes tinned or fresh, we would make pizzas, if we didn't have yeast then we made scone dough minus the sugar and this worked perfectly well. We would roll it out the size of the baking tray normally a 20x10x2 inches. With the tomatoes we had scrounged or acquired we would chop the luncheon meat into small dice, mix it all together and spread it out over the tray, some of us would get herbs and pepper from the main kitchen before the exercise started and we would sprinkle oregano on top, finally we would cover it with the compo grated processed cheese which was known to us squaddies as (cheese possessed). The ovens if we were lucky to have one were fitted onto the burner stand and the pizzas would be cooked in these, once cooked we would cut them up and serve them, perfect for lunch and the troops used to marvel at how we had managed to cook pizza with compo.

Here is a recipe to try at home this will make about four pizzas.

*****

Scone dough.

SR flour 10oz

Butter or marge 2 ½ oz

Water a small amount.

Salt

Toppings.

One small tin of chopped tomatoes.

One chopped onion lightly cooked and cooled.

Green or red peppers or both.

Oregano.

Plenty grated cheese

Mushrooms

Ham, pineapple, chicken, anchovy's, chilli, bacon, you can use absolutely anything you want to put on it or what you fancy, if you have anything left in the fridge put it on the pizza

*****

This is something you can just throw together and use any leftovers you may have in the fridge, I personally just like tomatoes, onions and grated cheese. The kids could help you make these too, but the best bit for me is the scone dough.

Mix the flour and butter and salt till you get a bread crumb texture then with a fork slowly add a drop of water till the mix comes together, remember slowly. It will leave the slides of the bowl clean and turn into a nice dough, don't over work it. Flour the board and flatten it out using your hands into one big circle, no need for the rolling pin or you can cut it into four individual bases and again flatten them out.

I cooked one in the halogen oven at 200 for 10 minutes and it is like shown in the photo

BEEF STEW WITH FARMHOUSE DUMPLINGS

When the troops were on the shooting ranges doing their personal weapon firing, they would be cold and hungry, the regiment always seemed to pick the winter months for this and when it was cold in Germany it would freeze the knackers off a brass monkey the tankies weapon was the SMG (Sub machine gun) not liked by a lot of people because of its inaccuracy especially compared with the SLR (Self-loading rifle). However, it did have its uses on exercise as the troops found numerous ways to open their beer bottles with it. The cold never stopped one man from finding the troops no matter where we were and that was Wolfgang's and his bratty van. Even on exercise with the tanks they would all be camouflaged and hidden from a potential enemy on radio silence, but not Wolfgang he could go places where a chieftain tank wouldn't dare venture. In fact, he would often know where the RV was before the officers were briefed. Some said he would have been a great asset to the German army during the war, as he would have made a fine map reader and his sense of sniffing the enemy out would have been a great advantage. He was a welcome sight for the blokes and within minutes of him pulling up there would be a queue of troops waiting for their bratwurst and chips, if I could go back in time, I would set up my own business just like Wolfgang he must be worth a bob or too now.

Anyway, back to the shooting ranges and the sound of the SQMSs Bedford pulling up was a sight for sore eyes, he would off load the hayboxes which contained lunch. The haybox worked similar to a flask only a lot bigger and inside was a six-gallon container full of steaming range stew at the side was a six-foot table with an urn of tea and loads off RAOC (Royal army ordinance corps) bread. The bread was in white waxy wrappers and never seemed to be fresh but this didn't deter the troops from taking half a dozen slices each.

'Right lads come and get it!' shouted the SQMS waving a half pint ladle in the air, 'This will stick to your fucking ribs like glue!'

They would queue up with their mess tins ready as the SQMS ladled it in like gruel, there was nothing like a mess tin full of thick stew on these freezing days and there wouldn't be much left.

Range stew was the name if it came from the central cookhouse but on exercise the tank crews would make their own and that would-be all-in stew. All in stew would mean anything in the compo went into the pot, meat, vegetables, sausage, beans, bacon burgers, chicken, oatmeal blocks even jam and cheese, I have also heard once that they put puddings into it. The funniest thing I saw was on exercise and a tank crew sat round a container of this stew which was keeping hot on a hexamine cooker, at the side of the cooker was a loaf of bread, all four of them covered in oil and grease picking bread out of the packet and dipping it into this concoction, once the bread had been devoured they would grab their spoons and eat the stew, now that's what I call sharing and it is a true story. When I was in the Falklands in 1983, we were on full compo rations apart from the usual potato's, eggs and flour and the compo margarine was perfect for making dumplings, this margarine was great for cooking with but once it was on a slice of bread for a sandwich it was like eating lard. Anyway, we would have stew and dumplings on the menu most days for one of the choices, we were feeding about 150 people and as long as we got a good selection of compo packs with different menus, we could put 3 or 4 choices on for lunch and evening meal. We tried to garnish the food up as best we could even though it was compo, I remember we used to go out the back of the kitchen and pick the greenest grass so we could chop it up to substitute fresh parsley. Just one more thing and it was before my time, one of the compo packs apparently had Irish stew in it, I never saw or tasted it but have been told it was very good, just thought I would mention it.

My beef stew is cooked in the slow cooker, and the dumplings are fluffy and flavoured with onions and bacon and parsley to give them a lovely savoury taste, perfect for winter days, here's how.

For four people.

*****

Lean diced beef 500g.

Two chopped onions.

Two celery sticks chopped.

Two bay leaves (optional)

Thyme (optional)

Two large carrots peeled and diced.

Potatoes peeled and diced 500g.

Small swede peeled and diced.

Salt and pepper

Gravy granules.

(For the dumplings)

Atora suet 2oz.

Sr flour 4oz.

Salt.

Drop of water.

One whole sweated onion.

One packet of bacon lardons or chopped bacon

Parsley

*****

Turn on the slow cooker.

Season and seal the beef well and put it in the slow cooker.

Fry the onions, carrots, celery and swede in the beef residue, add a pint of water and bring back to the boil, thicken with the Bisto granules pour onto the meat, add the bay leaves and thyme(optional) put the lid on and leave for about four hours, you can put the diced potatoes in if you wish but I like to put them in for the last hour or so then they don't disintegrate, however if you use baby potato's you should be okay.

In a frying pan cook the onions and bacon lardon till medium brown let them cool.

In a bowl mix the flour suet and salt then add the cold onions and bacon, very slowly add the water till the mixture leaves the side of the bowl clean. Don't overwork the dough cut it into four and put them on top of the stew, cook for another hour. If like us you like your dumplings then double up on the recipe and make eight of the little beauty's. Fantastic easy grub for the winter days ahead.

CHICKEN AND MUSHROOM PIE

Short crust pastry

*****

Plain flour 6oz.

Butter 1 ½ oz.

Lard 1 ½ oz.

Salt water to bind.

Filling.

One large chicken breast diced into chunks.

A dozen button mushrooms quartered.

One large onion chopped.

Butter about 2oz.

One tablespoon of plain flour.

88

Milk a small amount.

Salt and pepper.

*****

You can make it in a flan ring or use some tinfoil pie cases, I got a pack of ten for about 50p.

Gently fry the chicken, mushrooms and onions till cooked, do not brown. Add the flour and stir in then slowly add the milk you need a nice thick consistency too thin is no good, cook the flour out for one minute, add the salt and pepper to taste then let the mixture cool.

In a bowl rub the butter, lard, salt and flour till you get the breadcrumb texture, then using a fork slowly add the water in droplets you will know when it's enough, don't overdo it or you will end up with a sticky messy batter, if you make a massive cock up of it then do it again, it's only flour and fat after all. Otherwise add the droplets of water then once it binds stir with the fork till it leaves the bowl clean. Don't over work the pastry put it in a dish and cover with cling film then put it in the fridge for half an hour.

With a knife cut off one third of the pastry and save for the tops.

The other two thirds divide into four and roll each piece out place it on the greased pie case and press the edges make sure it overlaps the edges. If you are not very good at rolling pastry it is easier to use these smaller tinfoil cases than a larger pie tin.

Use all the filling as shown in the photo, then divide the remaining pastry into four pieces and roll out for the tops, you will need some egg wash for the edges. Once you get the tops on cut off the surplus pastry and crimp. Put a knife slit in the top to let the steam out and egg wash, I was a bit posh and with the leftover pastry I made some little leaves then I egg washed again, I will hold my hands up now because if any of my chef friends are reading this they will pull me for putting leaves on a chicken pie, leaves are for fruit pies only hehe, but I don't care this is my book.

I cooked these in the oven at 150 for about 35 to 40 minutes without over browning them, so as I keep saying keep your eye on them, when I am using the oven myself I have a timer and I just set it for every ten minutes to remind me to look, that is old age for you.

SEEDY'S YORKSHIRE PARKIN

I really love parkin especially when it is sticky and stodgy that is why it is in my top 50 favourites. I used to make it a few weeks before bonfire night every year when I was working then seal it in a tin until I needed it. best to use oatmeal but I have tried it with porridge oats which I zapped in the blender, one year I even tried ready brek but it turned out a bit dry. Oatmeal was difficult to get hold of in the army kitchens so we often used the breakfast porridge oats it wasn't the same but it was all we had at the time. Seedy Simpson came up with a fantastic idea and that was to use the surplus oatmeal blocks from the compo that had accumulated in the ration store from previous exercises, even the master chef was curious about this one shaking his head and saying it wouldn't work. Anyway, Seedy was undeterred and opened all the tins of oatmeal blocks and crushed them into fine crumbs watched closely by the chef.

'It won't work Simpson,' said the master chef smiling,' You can't make parkin without oatmeal.'

After preparing the black treacle, syrup, butter and other ingredients he used the oatmeal block crumbs in place of the breakfast oats. As I said earlier in this book oatmeal blocks had the taste of dry flap jack and were delicious with jam and cheese, so I was looking forward to tasting Seedy's

Parkin. When it was cooking the sweet smell engulfed the cookhouse it was gorgeous. I have to say when I had a slice it was spot on with a lovely toffee like edging, even the master chef complimented Seedy on this creation, it was sticky, gingery and had a gorgeous taste of flap jack.

I was a bit dubious myself when I did this recipe using Hob Knobs for this book but it works and I am on my third batch now, remember for this recipe make sure you measure the ingredients accurately, lets recreate this delicious parkin and I want you to try it too so here goes.

Serves eight.

*****

Soft butter 110g

Soft dark brown sugar 110g

Black treacle 55g

Golden syrup 200g

Hob knobs crushed 225g (or the traditional oatmeal).

SR flour 110g

Ground ginger two teaspoons

Eggs 2 beaten

Milk one tablespoon

Pinch salt

*****

Preheat the oven 120 to 140 grease and line the tin with greaseproof.

In a pan gently heat the butter, sugar, treacle and golden syrup don't allow it to get too hot just warm it through to melt the butter, (I put mine in a bowl in the micro wave for 30 seconds). Remove from the heat.

Sift all the dry ingredients make a well and pour in the butter mixture and eggs and milk and combine together.

Pour in the tin and bake for 1 ½ hours, I used the halogen oven on 120 as I find it is quick and accurate after half an hour I turned it down to 110, once cooked I put the cake on a rack to cool before wrapping it in foil and storing in a tight tin, delicious and another fantastic idea from my old friend Seedy Simpson, try it you won't be disappointed.

When you use the oven keep your eye on the parkin, if you think it is browning too quick then turn the oven down slightly.

CHICKEN VOL AU VENT

This is a classic for the compo and if any of my ACC cook colleagues are reading this, they will remember doing this on exercise either a chicken pie with the rough puff pie topping or an adventurous chicken vol au vent. No problem here with the compo ingredients the rough puff was made with the lardy margarine and the chicken supreme was already in the tin, it was just a matter of making 50 vol au vents bases, it was always better if were in a static location for a few days then we would have time to do them. The only problem with rough puff pastry was that it didn't rise as good as the proper made stuff but it did work, we would have to use the empty compo tins as cutters for the pastry. Chicken supreme was normally served with the compo Patna rice, the rice was easy to cook as I soon found out, one tin of rice to two tins of water, add salt and bring to the boil then take of the heat and cover, we gave it a stir after 20 minutes and it was perfect. As you have read in my other recipes, we would often wash the sauce off a few of the chicken flavoured meals and egg and breadcrumb or batter the meat it was a bit of a balls ache but it allowed us to do different things.

Seedy came up with an idea of cooking the rice then chopping the washed chicken up just saving one tin with supreme sauce to bind it all together. He mixed it with the rice and added a few egg yolks, then using the POM (mashed potato powder) for dusting we would portion them up and shape them into these rice and chicken cakes, then we would fry them. They were not as popular as some of the compo concoctions we made but Seedy was always up for a new challenge, when it came to compo, when it came to sex, he thought he was a god. I will never forget when we went to Hamburg in the early 80s and the famous peep show incident which we often talked and laughed about, these peepshows consisted of about 20 cubicles in a circle and at the centre of the circle was a revolving bed with a bird stripping for all the cubicles to view, as we squeezed into these cubicles there was barely enough room to turn around. You would shut the door and there was a coin slot that you put your money in, once you did this the metal screen would lift up slowly allowing you to see the woman through the glass screen, the woman was on a rotating bed seductively getting her kit off. Seedy in his wisdom and being a Yorkshire man decided we should both get into one cubicle together to save money. We were like contortionists trying to get our bodies to fit in this small space but we both finally got in and closed the door. Then we were fumbling about trying to get the money out of our pockets to put in the coin slot. Trembling with excitement Seedy finally found the slot and inserted the coin. The screen went up and our two slavering faces and noses were pushed up against the glass as we glared at this bird who was stripping on the bed. As the bed rotated her smiling seductive face soon turned to horror as she saw these two squashed faces staring at her, what a sight we must have looked. She jumped up and she shouted to the bouncers who came running to the cubicle and dragged us out, me and Seedy must have been the first squaddies ever banned from a peep show.

You can either make your own vol au vents or just buy them from the supermarket which is probably cheaper, I had some puff pastry left so decided to use that and cut my own out.

For four Vol-au-vents

*****

Vol-au-vents 4

One large chicken breast diced up.

Onions 2 chopped up.

Mushrooms a dozen chopped or sliced.

Fresh cream.

Thick bechamel sauce

Salt and pepper.

Cook the vol-au-vents for 10 minutes at 170

94

Seal the chicken onions and mushrooms and season.

Make a very small amount of my bechamel I used a teaspoon of butter and flour to make my roux, add the cream slowly till you get a smooth thick consistency cook for one minute stirring all the time. It is very important to keep it thick so you can pile plenty in the vol-au-vents. Add the cooked meat, onions and mushrooms to the sauce and stir.

Put plenty into each vol-au-vent as shown then put the pastry lids back on keep them warm and serve. Very easy to do both at home and in the field, plus they look good.

.

BEEF WELLINGTON

This is another one of my favourite top 50 recipes a bit expensive but you have to use fillet steak for the best results, the nearest we could get to this recipe with compo was poor mans stewed steak or chicken pasties. I remember one day on zero hotel, the officers mess mobile restaurant and I came up with the idea of trying to make puff pastry in the field, all I needed was the flour and the compo margarine which was perfect for this pastry because it had a similar texture to pastry margarine. I made the pastry folding it numerous times as you do with puff pastry and it worked, it was perfect for pie tops and pasties. I once took the apples out of the apple pudding and made apple turnovers on the mess truck.

"How the hell did you make these Alice?' said the CO (commanding officer), 'I thought we were on compo rations.'

I told him what I had done, how I made the puff pastry and where I got the apples from. I had made about a dozen of these turnovers and was saving them till the evening dinner but the CO had other ideas.

'The CO wants you to cut them in half Alice,' said the mess caterer, 'And could you serve them up at the briefing in ten minutes.'

The mess caterer was normally a staff sergeant or sergeant major who would keep all the mess staff on their toes.

I got the silver trays put a doyley on them then I laid out the pieces of the apple turnover on the platters, the waiter served them up to the amazed officers with a glass of wine as they filtered into the penthouse briefing tent. I could hear them whispering "Where did they get these from? They taste amazing" as they tucked into the turnovers. After the briefing the CO told the mess caterer how impressed he was with my inventiveness in making these pastry's and decided that he would like a dinner night in the field before the exercise finished and yes he wanted filet de boeuf en croute "Beef Wellington" of course they had to buy the beef fillet out of the officers daily messing from back at main camp, but the CO insisted that I made the compo margarine puff paste but to keep the dinner as compofied as possible. The dinner was a lavish affair to say the least, two six-foot tables were put together lengthways, two white sheets served as the tablecloths. I remember there were about a dozen of them for the meal mainly the hierarchy of the regiment, a gleaming candelabra with red candles was set in the centre of the table with regimental silver at each side of it all cleaned and polished by the regimental Silverman, white napkins were professionally folded by the mess caterer and his waiters, the regimental place mats, cutlery and crystal glasses were inch perfect using a tape measure and in front of the cutlery were green canvas chairs. Gleaming silver ashtrays were dotted about on the side tables, there was a hessian mat covering the grass floor and even a door mat to wipe their feet before they came in. I have to say that in the middle of nowhere it looked fantastic, the meal consisted of Mock turtle soup (another compo classic) with my fresh bread rolls, mock turtle was one five or six powdered compo soups that came in the packs, this was followed by the beef wellington with my compo margarine puff pastry, I had acquired some field mushrooms and onions to make my duxelles stuffing for the beef, sauté potatoes and compo peas. I made a cowboy madeira sauce using the oxtail soup and madeira wine. For the pudding I made rice condes with the compo rice pudding and fruit salad, I made a cornflour glaze with the fruit juice and for a few tins of jam and marmalade I got some fresh cream from a local German farmer. It was a success and the only thing that was bought was the beef fillet the rest was composite. The waiters did their professional silver service for the officers and the only thing that was missing was the regimental band, nothing was wasted the ends of the beef that were left over were eaten by the deserving mess staff and the wine dregs were drunk by me. Some would say it was extravagant to have a dinner like this in the field when all the regiment were on compo, but to be fair they did buy their own beef. When we eventually got back to civilisation, I used to tell people who just shook their heads in disbelief, especially if I tell my civilian friends these days, I loved it because it was so typically British officer style, it was like being on the set of Downton Abbey. The recipe below is how I cooked it on that particular exercise, however for this I bought the puff pastry.

For two people.

*****

One or two fillet steaks.

Oil for frying. Salt and pepper.

Puff paste (shop bought)

Egg wash.

Two very thin pancakes to wrap the beef and stuffing, from my cheese and onion pancake batter recipe just a small amount though.

(Duxelles stuffing).

One onion roughly chopped.

Ten button mushrooms roughly chopped.

A little butter to sweat the onions and mushrooms.

One or two slices of dry bread for breadcrumbs.

(Madeira sauce). I made a thick Bisto for the base

Small onion finely chopped.

Six finely sliced button mushrooms.

Salt and pepper.

Madeira wine ¼ of a cup. If you haven't got it put a drop of sherry in.

One mug of made up Bisto gravy thickened, if you want to make a proper demi-glace you can but for me this works just as well

Drop of heavy cream(optional)

First of all, remove any sinew from the fillet then season the steaks with salt and pepper, heat the oil up and seal the steaks well on both sides put on a plate to cool, if you like them rare quickly seal them, as I have to eat this I like mine well done so I cooked it for two minutes each side

Meanwhile if you have processer zap the bread into crumbs, finely chop the onions and mushrooms.

Melt the butter and gently cook the onions and mushrooms until all the liquid has evaporated, add a quarter of the Bisto gravy, stir well season and bring to the boil, add the breadcrumbs you need a nice thick stuffing consistency, let it cool.

If you have bought the puff paste it should be quite thin, cut two large squares ready to go I only did one steak. First lay the thin pancake out and put the cold duxelles in the centre, put the sealed steak on top and wrap up in the pancake as tight as you can without splitting it, you can do it without the pancake but it holds the filling better. Next put the pancake parcel on the puff pastry and wrap this up too using the egg wash to seal the edges. Turn the whole thing over and put on a greased tray, decorate with spare bits of pastry and egg wash again. Pop in the oven at 200 for 45 minutes, cover with foil after 30 minutes to prevent the pastry over browning or turn the oven down, when done leave to stand for 5 minutes before cutting or serving, the one I cooked above will do for two people. If you want to make your own puff pastry try this.

*****

Plain flour 8oz

½ teaspoon salt

Unsalted butter 9oz cold but not rock hard.

¼ pint of ice-cold water.

Sift the flour and salt in a bowl.

Cut the cold butter into cubes.

Stir the butter into the flour using a table knife ensuring you coat every piece.

Pour in the water and bring everything quickly together to get a rough dough.

Flour your work surface and roll the pastry out into an oblong till it is about 1cm thick, straighten up the sides with your hands now and again.

Fold the bottom third of the pastry up then the top third down, press the open ends of the pastry with the rolling pin. Roll out and do the same again, repeat, four times then cover and chill in the fridge preferably overnight.

This is what we called rough puff pastry as it is easier to make, it is rewarding if you get it right but for me the shop bought stuff is better and easier, have a go though.

LEFTYS WELSHRARTERBIT

This was one of the compo lunch choices that was staring us in the face but nobody could see it apart from my old friend Lefty Wright. Back in the main camp kitchen we would make it for lunch with a strip of bacon across and a couple of slices of tomato garnish then grill it, sometimes we would put a poached egg on top and it would become buck rarebit.

'Welsh rarebit!' said Lefty drinking his Paderborn pils around the number one burner, 'Everyone stared at him.'

'What?

'Welsh rarebit for lunch,' he said, 'We could make it with Paderborn pils.'

Basically, it is cheese on toast to us commoners but a bit posher as it is made with a thick bechamel made with stout, mustard, cheese and spread onto a slice of bread ready for the for the grill or in our case the field oven and we had all the ingredients in the compo. It is something that is so simple it completely bypassed us as we sat around the burner night after night talking. It was the same for me, on the officer's mess truck Zero hotel. I found it was very hard to think of unique things to do with the compo, then I came up with a belter "Croque Monsieur" it is a French baked or fried boiled ham and cheese sandwich, I think we would call it a toasty hehe. I used a cutter on the slices of

101

bread, compo cheese and luncheon meat to get perfect circles of each, then I sandwiched the cheese and luncheon meat in the bread rounds and dipped it in egg and fried it in the compo margarine. I served it to the officers as a savoury and they loved it.

'Paderborn pils?' I said.

'Well we don't have any stout,' said Lefty waving his bottle, 'So I will make it with this.'

So, the next day Lefty made a roux with compo margarine and flour and used the Paderborn pils as stock, he then put loads of the famous cheese possessed in and let it cool. The RAOC (Royal army ordinance corps) bread was on the turn anyway so Lefty spread the cooled mixture thickly on the bread, instead of bacon which we didn't have we put a little slice of bacon grill on for garnish then in the oven to brown, they are better if they are grilled under a salamander, but for us in the middle of a muddy wood there was no such thing. Lefty's rarebits were a success another good compo choice to add to our repertoire. On our boozy nights around the number one burner we often joked how we could write a book about compo.

For four people.

Four slices of bread (I am using my homemade bread for this)

Grated cheese.

Mustard powder.

Milk or stout, I am using (Old Peculiar) Guinness is best you only need half a can then you can drink the rest, if you don't want stout in your rarebit use milk.

MANCHESTER TART

I know a lot of you will remember this dessert from your school days I certainly do and what about the semolina they used to serve us accompanied with prunes? Or the pink custard with jam roly poly. Manchester tart was another army desert that could be knocked up quickly as a cold pudding, I can remember the thick pastry, we would smother it in jam then we would put the leftover custard from tea the day before over it. Finally, we would give it a generous sprinkling of desiccated coconut before portioning it up for the evening tea meal, funnily enough it was always quite popular and was one of the first things to go.

Can it be done with compo I hear you say? Well the answer is yes and I have done it, I did need the added ingredient of custard powder though. The oatmeal block was similar to flap jack type of texture and we used to put them in a container and crush them with the end of a rolling pin, we would melt the compo marge and mix it with the crumbs, are you getting the picture? We would press the biscuit base into the 20x10x2 and cover with the compo jam. Next, we mix the compo dried milk with the water bring it to the boil and thicken with the custard powder, add the sugar. Finally pour the custard over the biscuit and jam base. You're probably thinking that we cheated by using custard powder which wasn't in the compo, but without all these little add-ons compo menus would have been boring and there would have been no fun in cooking in the field.

My wife Mandy kindly got me the fancy little flan cases amongst a lot of other things for this book, they look very professional but you can use a normal flan ring or shallow dish, my only advice is don't make them too deep or the custard will collapse when you try and portion them onto the plates, I would say definitely no more than an inch of custard in thickness. I used the sweet pastry from the apple pie recipe and got eight flan bases.

For eight tartlet flans.

*****

Sweet pastry.

Fresh cream.

Jam.

Glace cherries.

Custard powder, I used two packets of bird's instant.

Small tin of evaporated milk.

Sugar extra 4 tablespoons.

Desiccated coconut.

*****

Line the flan cases or whatever you are using and cook blind at 140 to 160 for 10 minutes they need to be a pale biscuit brown.

I used two packets of the instant custard that was enough to make 1 ½ pints but I only needed about a pint so I boiled ¾ of a pint of water made the custard it was thick so then I added the small tin of evaporated milk which gave me the consistency I wanted, add the sugar then if you still think it is a little thick put a drop of milk in. If you make four flans, you will only need half that custard.

Once the flans have cooled put half a teaspoon of jam in each one and spread it over the base, then carefully spoon in the custard as much as you can without going over the edges. Of course, you can use proper bird's custard powder but just make sure you keep it thick, don't be tempted to use the tinned custard it won't work, put the flans in the fridge to set.

Whip the double cream you need about ½ pint, then pipe onto the top of each tartlet, if you are no good at piping then put a dollop on them instead using a couple of teaspoons, scoop the cream on one and use the other to push it onto the tartlet, finish with a glace cherry and sprinkle with desiccated coconut. That's it jobs a good un.

STEAK PUDDING

    This book is about all my favourite recipes and something I am not too keen on is offal so you won't see any in this book but if you want to add diced kidney to this recipe feel free, just cook it with the beef. So why have I put steak pudding in my top fifty I hear you say? Well the answer is I used to love the compo steak and kidney pudding which came in the E pack and it was the only time I ever ate kidney. I can remember cooking kidneys for the officers for breakfast they would have them sautéed in butter with salt and pepper and the smell used to turn my stomach, worse still if I came in with a hangover. For the compo steak and kidney, we would open the tin at both ends and push the pudding out, it was covered in a white suet like pastry and we would cut them in half and put them on the 20x10x2 baking trays and cover them with gravy ready for the oven. They were called baby's heads by us squaddies because that is what the soft suet pastry resembled, there wasn't a great deal more we could do with these regarding catering apart from the famous all in stew. Seedy Simpson came up with an idea though and that was to pipe a large rosette of (POM) compo mashed potato on top, it was different and resembled a steak and kidney cottage pie. Apart from that there wasn't much we could do with them; they were just steak and kidney puddings or babies heads. I am going to make steak and mushroom pudding you can add some diced kidney when you seal the beef off. These little puddings are a treat and are so easy to make, not only that you can put them in the slow cooker before you go to work and forget about them. This is another recipe I am cooking on location in Lingdale (my holiday) so I am not in my familiar surroundings, but the food tastes so much better when you have had a brisk walk on the beach in the sea air.

Suet pastry for four puddings

*****

SR Flour 8oz

Atora suet 4oz

Pinch of salt.

Water

Stir the suet into the flour with a fork then very slowly add cold water by the drops till it leaves the bowl clean and you get a nice dough. I used my little pudding basins again, don't forget I am cooking these in a slow cooker or a pan with a lid, unless you have a pressure cooker.

The filling lean diced beef 200g

If you want to put kidney in this then share the weight diced kidney 100g, beef dice 100g.

Seasoned flour.

Mushrooms.

Two chopped onions.

Salt and pepper. Bisto for thickening.

Yes, I use a lot of Bisto, but why make the job hard? When you can achieve the same results, the taste is the same you have still got all the lovely meat juices so nothing is wasted. Of course, you are free to add plain flour to the sealed meat, a bit of tomato puree, water and a stock cube and thicken it the correct way, as I say the taste is all that matters.

Seal the beef in seasoned flour add the onions, mushrooms and half a pint of made up Bisto gravy, put in the slow cooker till tender it needs to be nice and thick but not solid so it holds up when the pudding is cut, leave to go cold.

Lightly grease the pudding moulds, cut 2/3rds of the pastry and then cut it into four, roll each piece out about an 8th of an inch, you need it to

107

carefully press it into the mould making sure you keep it at the correct thickness, overlap it over the rim for sealing later.

Fill the puddings to the top with the cooked meat then wet the edges with a pastry brush, cut the remaining pastry into four and roll out topping each pudding, seal and trim with a knife, cover with lightly buttered tin foil and seal the foil onto the rim all the way round, put into the slow cooker with boiling water three quarters up the pudding and forget about them. These puddings should just drop out of the moulds when they are done providing you have greased them correctly; I like to cook the meat first and get it tender that is just my preference. When I did these in training, we had to put the raw meat and onions into the pastry with a bit of salt and pepper put the tops on and steamed them for a few hours, the meat was still tender but I like mine to have a thick gravy. When they are cooked turn them out onto a plate and cut into them, watch the lovely tender beef flow out onto the plate as shown in the photo, they are delicious with mash, mushy peas and mint sauce, proper Yorkshire grub.

BAVAROIS

     I made these for the first time in years last weekend when I was called to my wife Mandy's workplace to cover for the chef while he was on holiday, firstly for those that are wondering I am afraid that I cannot make these with compo rations as I am not god, so as much as I would like to give you the magic compo recipe for bavarois I cannot. However Seedy (sex mad) Simpson came up with one of the most ludicrous cowboy methods I have ever seen, it was on a snowy exercise on Soltau west Germany and he decided to mix the compo dried milk with water brought it to the boil and thicken it with cornflour, after stirring the sugar in he poured the mixture into pudding basins, covered them and put the basins in the snow to set. Nothing at all like a bavarois, Seedy's was more like a cheap blancmange hehe, once they were set he would turn them out onto a tray, you could hear the plop of suction as they fell out of the pudding basin like something dropping into the swill bin, then he surrounded these culinary delights with the compo tinned fruit salad, Seedy thought they looked great of course, he had a big smile on his face at his achievement as he put a cherry from the fruit salad on top of each of the watery, milky, blancmanges wobbling them in front of him like a pair of white tits. Needless to say, the lads still ate it amazed at the magic we could perform in the field with the army ration packs. Seedy could make John Wayne look like an amateur cowboy, get on yer horse Seedy hehe.

This recipe below uses sugar, egg yolks, cream and gelatine. But they taste so much better than the packet garbage you buy in the supermarket. Last weekend I did mine with summer berries and I thought they looked fantastic, I love to make my food look good, for me it is half the battle, I hate to see sloppy efforts in food presentation and it's the little things that I pick up on, for example if we go out for a meal and I get my main course and I see a small dribble of gravy or sauce on the edge of the plate I think that it is unprofessional, it should have been wiped off before it left the kitchen. We would have got the bollocking of our lives if the master chef had seen any unnecessary gravy or custard splashes on the plate that we were serving to the troops. You may think that is a bit harsh but that's how we were taught, the learning process in the military is quite simple, you do something wrong, then comes the bollocking and extras and eventually you learn and you don't do it again. Sometimes I boil eggs for our salads at home often without timing them properly and when I shell and cut them, they are dark around the yolks because they have been cooked too long, I often reprimand myself under my breath "Oh fucking hell Alice" I remembered how the master chef would have reacted had he seen it.

Before I show you the bavarois let me tell you a little story about a blind man who was in the old folks home where I once worked when I first left the army, he used to take most of his meals in his room, I would always ensure that is tray was set up correctly and that is food was garnished whether it be breakfast, dinner or tea, he was a slow eater but he did manage to eat it himself. Some staff would say to me why are you bothering to do that? He cannot see it's a waste of time. I told them it is my job and if I was in that poor fellows' predicament, I would expect the same kind of service whether I could see it or not. When he died his daughter came to the kitchen to thank me for everything that I did for him. Sometimes she would be there when his meals arrived and she would sit and explain to him what was on his plate and how nice it looked, she was so impressed that I had garnished all her father's food for him even though he was blind, a lovely compliment for doing my job, something I do now without thinking.

For four bavarois.

*****

Double cream 200ml.

Vanilla essence or preferably a vanilla pod.

Castor sugar 50g.

Three egg yolks.

Strawberry's for decoration.

Double cream for decoration.

110

Strawberry jelly mix (optional)

Gelatine (I used Dr Oetker gelatine from Asda rather than mess about with gelatine leaves, the gelatine powder is easy to use just follow the instructions.)

If you want to be chefy like me put some fruit in the bottom of the pudding moulds as shown then pour some strawberry jelly over the fruit, you don't have to do this its optional but it looks good when turned out, pop them in the fridge for half an hour to set.

Prepare the gelatine as instructed and let it cool, not too cool or it will set.

Meanwhile put the cream onto boil with a tablespoon of the caster sugar, keep your eye on the cream while you put the egg yolks, rest of the sugar and vanilla essence in a bowl whisk till it becomes white and creamy, slowly pour the cream onto the egg yolk mix whisking all the time. Pour back into the pan and return to the stove for a few minutes you will see it thicken like a custard, add the gelatine mixture and carry on whisking till it is cooler, be careful if it gets too cold it will start to set. Take the pudding moulds from the fridge and pour the cool mixture into them, if you are not putting fruit or jelly in the bottom it is okay, but if you have put jelly do make sure that the mixture is cool or it will melt the jelly, its good fun but it looks good as you can see.

SALMON EN CROUTE

The last and first time I did this was for the Duchess of Kent when we were in Detmold, the CO (Commanding Officer) of the regiment came into the clothing store and asked me if I would like to cook for the Duchess. At first, I thought he was taking the piss but he wasn't smiling and the QM was stood behind him looking quite serious. I accepted and felt honoured, the last time I had cooked was the year before in Cyprus when the cooks had asked me to stand in for them while they went to a darts match piss up. The CO ran through the menu it was for six people including the duchess starting with cold soup Vichyssoise followed by salmon en croute and finished with lemon sorbet, a simple menu indeed and I have never been so nervous in all my life about feeding so few people.

When the day finally arrived I set off to the COs house which was actually situated on the barracks, I remember the security around the house with the duchesses' private bodyguards who gave me strange looks as I approached the house carrying my knife bag, I showed them my ID then they searched me. I remember that this was just a flying visit for the duchess but even so the security on camp was always stepped up when she came and every car had to be removed from outside all the accommodation blocks and parked on the main square, any cars not moved would be towed away. The guard would be doubled and the dog handlers would be patrolling the camp too. Once I had been frisked, they let me through to the front door where I was greeted by the COs wife who looked a bit flustered and anxious.

'Thank god you are here Alice,' she said, 'What a day it's been.'

She had been panicking all day that everything was going to go alright, she took me into her kitchen and spoke quietly.

'Everything you asked for here,' she said, 'But watch out, that damn lady in waiting is a bloody nuisance with her interfering, she has been in and out all day asking this and asking that, it was like she was watching my every move.'

'Okay,' I said starting to get things together, the COs wife left me to it.

'The duchess is upstairs with her entourage, I will be in the dining room if you need me Alice then I will be off to get ready myself,' she said.

I started to get everything prepared which took me about an hour, this left me about an hour or so before service the waiters had arrived to the relief of the COs wife so I thought I would pop out the back door for a smoke. A few minutes later the door opened and this posh bird came out clutching a cigarette case and lighter, she asked who I was and what I was doing, I explained to her that I was doing the dinner for the duchess and guests.

'My name is Penelope Calthorpe, lady in waiting to the duchess,' she said lighting a fag up, 'What is your name?'

'Alice,' I said.

'Alec?' she said.

'No Alice,'

'That's a strange name,' she said, 'You haven't had one of them operations, have you? You hear all sorts of things these days but I am open minded about it.'

'Oh no nothing like that,' I said, 'It's my nickname!'

'Oh of course,' she said looking embarrassed.

The COs wife came outside.

'Oh, there you are Alice,' she said, 'Are you all ready?'

113

'I am going to start cooking now,' I said walking back into the kitchen.

The lady in waiting followed me still red in the face. She wanted to see everything I was doing, it felt like she was checking to make sure I wasn't going to poison any of the duchess's food, plus I hate it when someone is staring over my shoulder. Once I got everything on the go, I went to help the COs wife who was still running around getting the dining table sorted. The meal went as well as could be expected and I did the washing up and cleaned the kitchen Penelope Tempest Calthorpe came back downstairs with the duchess's personal hairdresser his name was Pierre a very eccentric feminine man, his hair was parted in the middle typical stereotype hairdresser you see in the movies. Anyway, he introduced himself and he got chatting in general, he told me all about all the famous people he had met in his line of work. Actually I got on well with him and this Penelope bird during the course of evening, the COs wife had left me some beers and after the dinner finished, I sat with Penny and Pierre for a drink probably the first time I have had a drink with a posh bird and a so called celebrity hairdresser, she offered us a drink of her sherry in one of them little poxy glasses hehe, Pierre just took the glass and gently sipped it, I took one and supped it straight off. I was happy with my Herforder pils, perhaps I should have invited her and Pierre back to the squadron bar with me, that would have opened their eyes up.

I will never forget that night and just before I left the CO brought the duchess through to see me to thank me for the meal, the CO at the time could have had the pick of the chefs from the main cookhouse yet he came to the clothing store and asked me, I was honoured.

For two people

Two skinned salmon fillets.

Chopped parsley.

Cream cheese 200g.

One lemon juice and zest.

Salt and pepper.

Puff pastry shop brought 500g

Egg wash.

Mix the parsley, cream cheese, lemon juice, zest, salt and pepper together in a bowl,

Cut the puff pastry into squares bigger than the salmon fillet.

Place the salmon fillet on as shown.

Put the cream cheese, parsley on the pastry and on the fish as shown.

Egg wash around the edges then put the other piece of puff pastry on top seal the edges with a fork and start forming your fish shape as best you can, you don't have to be perfect as it will all puff up once in the oven.

Once it is done brush with egg wash and cook in the oven at 180 to 200 for about 25 minutes.

Once cooked take out of the oven and leave to rest for about 10 minutes, very good with baby mint potato's and a nice green salad with dressing. This is the exact recipe that I did for the Duchess of Kent that evening, she was very easy to cook for, but the pressure on me that night was immense for such a simple menu, have a go it tastes delicious

CRÈME CARAMEL

I love doing these they are a simple and a very delicate dessert that requires gentle cooking similar to crème Brulee only these are not as rich, the main thing is getting the caramel the correct colour. I first did these in basic training and I remember they puffed up like a souffle and were full of air bubbles the oven was too hot, I had overcooked them and got a bollocking from the chef instructor. They are best cooked in a baking tray with water nice and steady till they set, then when they are turned out the sides should be lovely and smooth with a lovely caramel colour on top. In a busy military kitchen, we would make ours with tinned milk and water maybe put extra eggs in to ensure they set properly. I actually cooked these on Zero hotel using savarin moulds I just omitted the caramel. Savarin moulds are like big doughnut rings ideal for making rum babas. Once the egg custard had been turned out I would fill the centre with the tinned compo fruit it was a simple idea but it worked and even better if I could scrounge some cream.

For four people.

*****

Caramel.

Sugar 3oz.

Water three tablespoons.

For the custard.

Three eggs.

Milk ¾ pint.

Sugar 1oz.

Vanilla essence one teaspoon full.

*****

Prepare the moulds grease lightly with unsalted butter, put them in a baking tin.

To make the caramel put the sugar and water on to the stove keep stirring till the granules disappear, stop stirring and boil till the sugar turns a dark copper colour.

Remove immediately from the heat to ensure the caramel doesn't burn and quickly pour into the four moulds, leave to cool and set.

Whisk the eggs, sugar, milk and vanilla essence and strain into a jug, before putting in the moulds, fill the baking tin to just over half way up the pudding moulds, then carefully place into the pre heated oven the oven 150, takes about 25 to 30 minutes till set don't let them brown.

Once they are set take them out of the oven and put the moulds onto a wire rack to cool then put them in the fridge. Once they are chilled carefully push the edges down with your finger then turn them upside down on a side plate and give them a quick shake you will hear them come loose, lift the mould and the custard should come out as above,

OXTAIL SOUP GERMAN

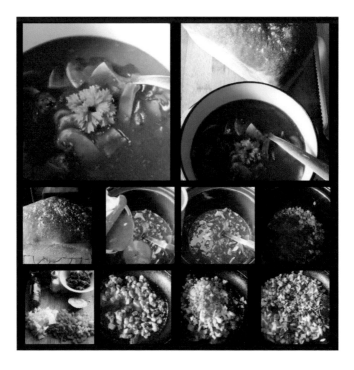

After having a skin full of German beer in the Bauernstube in Fallingbostel my last port of call before going back to camp was the Imbiss where they did a lovely bowl of oxtail soup with crusty brown bread even if half of it did go down my shirt, the Germans called it Ochsenschwanzsuppe. It was one of the tastiest soups I have ever eaten and I often think and crave for it, unfortunately I do not have a recipe for it in my memory although I have tried to replicate on numerous occasions. I remember making one when I was in training but it wasn't a patch on the German version, also to make oxtail soup from scratch can be a long job. Of course, today we have slow cookers and pressure cookers that make it easier especially when cooking the oxtail. In the good old compo ration packs, we had oxtail soup and on exercise we would use it for gravy and sometimes with help of the tinned stewed steak and compo veg mixed together would make an okay soup, well at least it tasted of oxtail. I think there were about four powdered soups, mock turtle, tomato, mushroom and chicken as well as the oxtail. Us cooks on exercise would often take some gravy browning from the main kitchen to colour these soups and use them for gravy. Another lovely soup we got in Germany was goulash, when we were skiing in Bavaria it was a good lunch time choice on the ski slopes a hot spicy

118

thick soup with large pieces of meat in it, served with a couple of slices of the lovely brown crusty German bread.

On the officer's mess truck especially in winter I used to do a goulash soup for lunch with my fresh bread. Back in the 70s we used to get tinned goulash in one of the packs for a compo meal it was served with rice, when the tin was opened the sauce was red with the paprika. I made the powdered oxtail soup in a large pan, sweated some chopped onions off, opened the goulash meat and put it all in the pot. The meat started to fall apart as it was so tender, I put a splash of sherry in and my concoction surprisingly tasted very nice, I served it up for lunch with my warm bread and the officers loved it.

Oxtail is still my favourite though, recently my sister went on a caravan holiday in Germany and brought me back four tins of Ochsenschwanzsuppe and as I ate them the memories came flooding back. This is a meal in itself, give it a go.

*****

One tin of Heinz oxtail soup.

Lean small diced 200g

Two whole chopped onions

A dozen sliced mushrooms

One large carrot peeled and cut into small dice.

A couple of celery stalks finely chopped.

Oil for frying

One beef stock cube.

Glass of red wine I used port

Salt and pepper.

Paprika a sprinkle on the sealing meat.

Half pint of thick Bisto.

To make oxtail soup you need to invest in the flavour and the flavour here is from the cooking time and the initial ingredients, the Heinz soup just gives it the oxtail taste. You can use prepared oxtails in place of the beef if you wish to make the flavour more intense, you would need to brown the oxtails first same as the beef.

I prefer my way as it is less hassle plus when you come in from work it is ready to eat.

119

Seal the beef in the oil with paprika till nice and brown, place in the slow cooker.

In the same pan put all the other ingredients apart from the Bisto and wine, sweat all the veg off then add the Bisto and stock cube, pour in the red wine and bring back to the boil. Put the whole lot in the slow cooker, season with salt and pepper, cover and cook on low for 4 to 6 hours.

If you do oxtails you will have to take them out and take the meat of the tail bone which after this amount of cooking time should drop off the ox tail.

Back to the beef which should now be lovely and tender and the vegetables apart from the mushrooms will have nearly disintegrated into the stock, open the Heinz soup and pour it in, just let it heat through and it is ready for serving as shown above. As much as I try, I will never get the taste of the oxtail soup I had in Germany all those years ago, but this is as near as damn it.

LEMONADE SCONES

This wasn't something I had planned for my book but sometimes cooking fascinates me and if I see an unusual recipe, I want to try it and not least this one. I have always had a good hand for making scones I must have made thousands in my time but when I saw these little beauty's I just had to give them a try.

We used to make loads of scones in the field using the basic scone mix below, they were quick and easy, Seedy came up with an idea to strain the juice off the fruit salad and chop the fruit up finer he added it to the dry mix, once the fruit was mixed into the dry mix Seedy added the strained juice from the cans to bring the dough together and it worked. Once they were cooked, they were spot on and when they were cut you could see the different colours of the fruit in the scone.

I remember in the mid-80s just before I left the army catering corps, I was on exercise with Zero hotel on Soltau, we had a special guest for afternoon tea which was the prime minister Margaret Thatcher. The regiment was on full alert at the time and all the Chieftain tanks were moved into what was called a box leger, for this the regiment would be formed up in a huge square of

121

armoured vehicles forming in essence a steel fortress and inside this fortress would be all the other regimental vehicles and slap bang in the middle was Zero Hotel where the PM would be having her afternoon tea, I remember the news headlines at the time "A ring of steel around the iron lady" or something similar to this. Now a lot of us squaddies were keen admirers of Mrs Thatcher at the time because she gave us good percentage pay rises. Afternoon tea was set up in Zero hotel consisting of freshly cut sandwiches assorted fruit cakes, fresh scones, cream and of course tea. The officers mess best crockery cups and saucers were out on show with silver teapots and spoons, the tent we were using was fitted with a hessian floor covering white table cloths covered the six-foot tables. For my first glimpse of the iron lady I was surprised at how small she was, she came in the tent with the CO, Adjutant and all the other hangers on. I was stood behind the cake table staring, the waiters were pouring tea into the china cups, in the distance was the mess caterer watching our every move in case we said or did something wrong. I recall her saying good afternoon to me, I didn't know whether to curtsy or bow hehe, I had heard so much about this lady it was hard to believe and now I was stood in front of her. She only had a cup of tea then within ten minutes she was gone. The next thing she was in the commander's seat of a chieftain tank tear arsing across Soltau with a huge pair of plastic goggles on, I can see that photo now which was in all the papers the next day.

Back in the army days and in the pastry department slab cakes, shortbreads ect, and especially scones were the easiest to produce so they were on the cake menu quite often, not by the master chefs doing but the cook that was in the pastry department. We always did maybe 20 or 30 of the harder cakes that were on the list, then topped them up with scones or slab cake or jam tarts which were easier and we could quickly make in bulk. The basic scone recipe below is tried and tested and it never fails me so if you don't want to make lemonade scones use this one. I have had the recipe in my head for years and I cannot remember if it is from MACs or not. the secret of a good scone is don't overwork the dough, I mix it quickly then roll it out and portion them with a round cutter I then turn them upside down and put them on a greased tray slightly touching each other, give them a quick brush with milk then in the oven at 200 for 10 to 15 minutes. First of all, let me give you my scone recipe which I have used for donkeys' years.

Basic scone mix.

Makes about 4 large scones.

*****

SR flour 10oz.

Lurpak butter 2 ½ oz.

Caster sugar 2 ½ oz

Milk to bind.

Sultanas, raisins, cherries whatever you fancy 2 ½ oz.

Pre heat the oven to 200 or 180 fan ovens.

Simply mix all the ingredients together and bind to a dough with the milk, remember do not over work. Put on a floured board and pat down to half an inch then cut them with a 2.5" cutter you don't really need to use a rolling pin, handle them as little as you can, brush with milk then cook for 12 to 15 minutes, once cooked put them on a rack to cool

*****

Lemonade scones

SR flour 450g

Double cream 250ml

Lemonade 250 ml

Caster sugar one tablespoon.

Milk to glaze.

Whipped cream for decoration.

Jam or lemon curd.

Pre heat the oven to 200 or 180 fan ovens. Combine the flour cream, sugar and lemonade in a bowl do not over mix it will make the scones dense, the dough should be soft and sticky. Turn onto a floured surface and gently pat down to about half an inch thickness. Using a 2.5" round floured cutter cut your scones out normally about 5 or 6 for this mix place on a greased tray. Then you may get another four from the off cuts.

Brush the tops with milk and bake for 12 to 15 minutes till golden, place on a rack to cool and serve with loads of cream and jam.

BRAISED STEAK

This is another of my favourite meals especially when it has been cooked for hours, you have probably seen my posts on facebook when I cook these steaks, you will notice too that I always stress to season and seal the meat. I wish I had a quid for the amount of bollockings and extra duty cooks I had when I was a young lad for not sealing the meat, I would have been a millionaire. Now when you have a hundred steaks to seal it can be a very tedious exercise and the thought of it would make us young cooks lazy by putting the steaks straight into a tray raw, pour the gravy over them, then cover them and put them in the oven before the master chef got back from lunch. We would then hope and pray that the master chef wouldn't notice them, come tea time we would tray and garnish them up and cover them with thick gravy to disguise them. The master chef would inspect the hotplate before the dining room doors were open and he would walk down the hotplate scrutinising the food.

'Who cooked this cauliflower?' he barked.

'I did chef,' said one of the young cooks.

'It's over cooked and there is water in the bottom of the tray,' he said, 'Take it away and strain the water off, don't let me see it again or else!'

'Yes chef!'

The young cook grabbed the insert out of the hotplate and went to strain the offending water off. Meanwhile the chef carried on his inspection.

'Who made the stew and dumplings?' he shouted.

'I did chef,' said Lefty Wright.

'What's that on the top Wright?' he said pointing to the floating oily mass.

'Dumplings Chef,' said Lefty.

'Don't take the fucking piss Wright you know what I mean!'

'Oil chef.'

'Enough fucking oily fat to fry chips in Wright, get it away and skim it off and take 4 extras.

'Yes chef.

Lefty scurried away with tray of stew and dumplings as the chef was looking at my steaks, he picked up the serving spoon and scraped the gravy of the steak I could see him shaking his head.

'Who did this!' he screamed.

'I did chef.'

'You didn't seal it did you Collins?'

'I didn't have time chef,' I said.

'You are duty cook you had all the lunch hour!'

'Sorry chef.'

'Seems like you are going to have a few more duty cooks Collins, take ten!' he shouted and moved on.

The thing was when he scraped the gravy off, he was looking for the browned meat from the sealing process and there wasn't any, I can assure you I never did it again. Even when I was working as a civilian chef, I would pick the cooks up for it.

For two people.

*****

Two nice braising steaks season with salt and pepper.

Two chopped onions.

Baton carrots and swede, feel free.

¾ pint of thick Bisto gravy.

Oil for frying.

Seal the seasoned steak till nice and golden, put in the slow cooker.

Fry the onions in the meat residue and half of the carrot and swede, I saved half for the garnish and presentation for this book otherwise you can put it all in. If I do this in the oven I just do exactly the same put it in a casserole dish cover and cook slowly about 100 to 120 for a few hours.

Put the Bisto gravy over the veg bring it back to the boil and then pour it over the steaks, put the lids on and leave all day, perfect if you are working or going out somewhere this is why I prefer it to the oven method. When you are ready spoon it out gently onto the plate as it is really tender, serve it with your favourite potatoes and veg. Before you eat your steak gently scrape the gravy off to check you can still see the singed brown sealing marks on the surface of the meat, if you can't I will be watching you.

INDIVIDUAL FRUIT FLANS

These little flans were suggested to me by my wife Mandy, she first saw them in the bakery section of Sainsburys, I decided to put it in my top fifty because we could make fruit flans with compo. There were about five or six compo desserts, rice pudding, mixed fruit pudding, apple pudding, ginger pudding and fruit salad, pears and peaches. I have covered a few of them already, fruit flans could be made by lining the 20x10x2 with sweet pastry made from the flour, marge and sugar, then we would blind bake it, cover the base with jam then strain the juice off the fruit salad and place it in the cooked pastry base, the juice would be boiled and thickened with cornflour and used as a glaze for the fruit. We could also make a fruit crumbles using the fruit which worked fine, once again Seedy Simpson came up with a great idea and decided to crush the oatmeal blocks and put a layer over the top of the crumble and when it was cooked it had a crunchy biscuit topping, another fantastic idea in its simplicity.

Four fruit flans.

You will need a batch of sweet pastry from my apple pie recipe.

*****

127

Jam.

Double cream.

Strawberry's

Packet of quick jell.

Divide and roll out the pastry, lay it in the flan rings and trim with a knife.

Blind bake at 140 to 160 for 10 minutes till biscuit brown.

Put jam in each flan, the arrange the strawberry's on top, make the quick jell as per the packet instructions and glaze the strawberries, finally finish with a rosette of double cream and a piece of strawberry. Very easy and they look great, just like you get in the shops.

FRESH BREAD

    This is one of the things I don't make much of these days, but it is on my list because years ago I loved to make it especially on the back of a Bedford in the middle of nowhere in a wood in Germany. The officers mess truck known as Zero Hotel the mobile restaurant and it was odds on that when it was out on exercise, I would be with it. Once we were parked up in the middle of a German forest the penthouse would be fitted to the side of the Bedford, then the whole lot would be camouflaged, it was a pain in the arse putting that netted nightmare up especially in the dark if it was raining. The penthouse as we called it would be the dining room and the briefing tent for the Commanding Officer, Squadron leaders and all the hangers on. Drinks would be served on silver trays like we were back in camp. The regimental silver would be put out on the white sheeted six-foot tables and even though we were on compo rations the regimental cutlery would be laid out in style. Silver salt and pepper pots, ashtrays and even the regimental candelabra was on display complete with burning candles, I can tell you now it was a sight to behold. On the back of the Bedford I would have two household cookers complete with gas bottles, one six-foot table to do my work on and another one for the bar staff. At the front of the Bedford were some shelfs where all the food and bar stock was stored, now I say food and we were on compo but this was zero hotel and I had a few more little luxury's and apart from flour I had potatoes, oil, butter, fresh veg, numerous herbs and spices, but my favourite was dried yeast.

Apart from the officers I also had to feed command troop I can't remember how many maybe twenty, but I had to feed them before the officers so in effect there were two sittings but they weren't allowed to use the penthouse so I fed them from the back of the Bedford. Once they were fed and watered then we would prepare for the officers, oh! and I almost forgot the RSM (Regimental Sergeant Major) who would come onto the back and sit at my preparation table to eat his meals. I had a good recipe for bread then and I am damned if I can remember it, it wasn't a MACs (manual of army catering) recipe I am sure of that, when I think about it these days I think the recipe was on the back of the dried yeast tin. Anyway, as soon as breakfast was done with and cleaned up, I would weigh the flour out and get the yeast fermenting, the mess caterer would make sure all the canvas flaps on the Bedford were tied down securely to keep the heat in, this was very important in ensuring a good batch of bread. Once I had mixed and kneaded the bread dough, I would cover it while I got the tins ready. The tins I used were charlotte moulds which were used for puddings back in the main camp officers mess, they were perfect because they were heavy and thin, I had quite a few of these and once greased I would knead the dough again before putting it into the tins to prove before finally going in the oven. As you can imagine it got a little bit hot on the back of that Bedford especially with both gas ovens on and the canvas flaps tied down. It would give me chance to have a couple of beers from the bar stock while I waited for the bread to prove.

'Are you alright in there Alice?' came the voice of the mess sergeant major from outside the canvas.

'I am fine sir,' I said nearly choking as I was taking a drink of beer at the time.

'Let us know when we can open the canvas flaps Alice,' he said.

'Okay sir it will be a while yet,' I said being very careful not to make a noise as I put the beer bottle on the table.

Talking of noise when the CO was holding his briefings in the penthouse all the mess staff were on the back of the Bedford, myself, barmen, waiters and we had to keep quiet, no talking, farting anything while the CO was doing his brief. I was waiting to serve dinner up and I can tell you it gets rather warm on the back of those Bedford's with the cookers on, we couldn't open a can of beer because the ring pull would make a sound when we opened it like Tshhh and if we did the mess caterer would give us a bollocking later. I found a cunning way to get around this ring pull and that was to get your nail under it ready to open and at the same time cough as you pulled it, to the officers in the briefing it sounded like an innocent cough but to us on the Bedford it was the nectar of the gods having a cool drink, after this the whole mess staff were at it coughing as we quietly drank our beers. As normal the briefing rolled on longer than usual and the coughing got more frequent as the beer took effect, by my sixth can I was losing my coordination between my cough and pull hehe, it was a distinct cough followed by the delay in the ring pull making it obvious what we were doing. After the meal the CO mentioned the coughing to the mess sergeant as the staff were clearing away, he told him it was due to the heat on the back of the Bedford making the air dry. The CO told him to make sure we get plenty to drink next time as it was interfering with his briefing, we were pissing ourselves trying not to laugh.

Anyway, back to the bread, I used to make about thirty or forty loaves per day and the aroma in the back of the truck was gorgeous. As soon as I had got all the bread in the oven, I would signal the mess sergeant major to untie the flaps and open up, the smell of the bread would then waft around our wooded camp site. Sometimes as soon as it came out of the oven there would be people milling around the Bedford by the tailgate wanting a slice of the warm bread with best butter and jam, they seemed to eat it as quick as I cooked it, talk about feeding the five thousand, it was hectic but making bread in those conditions was so satisfying. Once the word got around about my bread SSMs (Squadron Sergeant Majors) and SQMSs (Squadron Quartermaster Sergeants) would all seem to be visiting our location and it wasn't to see command troop. They would be stood with mugs of tea and chunks of bread with the officer's best butter and compo jam, the butter would be running down their chins from the warm bread. I used to enjoy all the fuss and amazement; they would often say to me "How the fuck did you manage to bake that bread on exercise Alice" I loved it. I don't think I have ever heard of any cook who made bread in the middle of the wood on exercise apart from me that is, perhaps I am wrong. I am know going to make some bread for the first time in maybe 40 years I will close my eyes when it is cooking and see if the smell takes me back to those happy busy days on the mess truck, I will have the lurpak butter and jam ready for when it is cooked.

Let's do it it's easy.

*****

Strong white flour 500g plus extra for dusting.

One tablespoons of salt.

Fast action yeast 7g.

Olive oil 3 tablespoons.

Water 300ml.

Mix the flour, yeast with the salt in a large bowl.

Make a well in the centre then add the olive oil and water, mix well together, if the dough seems a little stiff add another tablespoon or two of water.

Tip on to a lightly floured surface knead for ten minutes.

Once the dough is satin smooth place in a lightly oiled bowl and cover with cling film, leave to rise for one hour or until it has doubled in size.

Grease your loaf tin or tray, knock back the dough and as Seedy would say pull it, stretch it, punch it, get violent and get it out of your system then rest while you have a smoke hehe, you can either put it in a loaf tin or on the baking tray to prove for a further hour until doubled in size put a kitchen towel over them. Once proved dust the bread with flour and if you are baking on the tray like a cottage loaf cut a cross in it with a sharp knife.

Bake for 25 to 30 minutes 220 or 200 fan ovens.

Once cooked turn out onto a wire rack.

It is a long process mainly in the proving, but if you have time give it a go, the ingredients are cheap so if you make a cock up you can do it again. Good luck I am going to cut me a slice of warm bread. With all the scaremongering about food shortages when Brexit finally happens this recipe might come in handy hehe.

CORNED BEEF AND POTATO CAKES.

Another compo classic in my top 50 is Corned beef or to us squaddies Corned dog, which if I remember rightly was found in the B pack it was classed as a main meal but I think most of the tank troops would use it for sandwiches or buttys as we called them, but if they did use it for a meal it would be sliced up and served with mashed potato (pom) vegetables not a very appetising meal but that was all they had and in a war situation they would have had to take it or leave it. For us cooks though it was another versatile choice and could be made into corned beef Fritters, corned beef pie, corned beef hash or my recipe of corned beef and potato cakes. The corned beef fritters were easy we would cut it into slices, then egg and breadcrumb before frying them. Corned beef pie was straight forward and we even made it into a cottage pie. The corned beef hash would have been the most likely option for a tank crew if they wanted a hot meal. Seedy Simpson apart from being sex mad, was one of the most inventive chefs I have ever worked with and one night while we were sat around the number one burner drinking beer, smoking and chatting, Seedy was telling us about one of his depraved sexual fantasy's when for some reason he came up with pancakes Toreador, what this had to do with leather masks and whips I will never know. Now before you all go checking the internet, pancake

Toreador is an actual recipe and is nothing to do with sadomasochism, it probably has never been served up on a military exercise in Germany before though. Basically, it is a pancake filled with corned beef mixed with sweated onion, rolled up and placed in a serving tray covered with tomato soup and grated cheese and baked in the oven, the proper recipe is a bit more elaborate, but hey! this is compo on exercise and we thought it was a good idea at the time. Back to the corned dog and I have memories of a six gallon container half full of boiling water on the number one burner, we would add the POM (compo mashed potato powder) margarine, onions if we had them, salt and pepper and about 20 cans of chopped corned dog, a dozen eggs to bind it, then when it cooled we would make about 50 corned beef cakes for lunch or dinner. If we had the time we would egg and bread crumb them between us and fry them till golden brown, this was another good filling choice and the lads loved them. Sometimes it was like a competition for which of us cooks could come up with the most ingenious idea for the next meal, we were like pigs in shit.

These corned beef and potato cakes are another simple recipe that combines most of the ingredients above, corned beef is not as cheap as it used to be but still makes a nice tasty meal, and so do some of Seedy Simpson's stories.

For four portions.

*****

One tin of corned beef cut into small dice.

One red onion finely chopped and cooked gently in butter.

Paprika.

Potato's 8oz

Butter for the onions

Salt and pepper.

Egg yolks two.

Egg one.

Seasoned flour.

Breadcrumbs.

Peel and season and cook the potato's in a pan then strain make sure they are free from water and thoroughly dry, I put them back in the pan and back on a low heat to dry them for a few minutes, better still do them in the microwave with a tablespoon of water and cover with cling film for 5 minutes. Mash with a fork and let them cool.

Put the finely diced onions in a bowl with a tiny bit of butter cover with cling film and microwave for about 3 minutes, these too need to be dry. Let cool.

Once everything is cold add the onions, parsley, salt and pepper, paprika, egg yolks and a few bread crumbs to the potatoes and mix together, then add the corned beef it should be nice dry and pliable if not just add a few more breadcrumbs.

Cut into four then shape into large rounds, egg and breadcrumb then pat them gently into the cake shape as shown, cover and put them in the fridge for an hour.

Fry them in oil till they are golden brown, kids will love these with ketchup and chips.

135

MEAT AND POTATO PIE

This is a compo classic and most of the cooks that served in my era will have done this on exercise, tins of stewed steak from the A and C packs, loads of cooked diced potatoes and a nice thick pastry crust, perfect for those winter days on the Soltau training area in Germany. The one I am showing you is perfect with mushy peas and mint sauce proper Yorkshire grub and the pastry just melts in your mouth.

Not a subject for a cook book but I will tell you anyway, remember I mentioned to you earlier when we were out in the field we all had to go at some time or other, some people would try and wait days till we went into Reinselen camp for the showers, for others it was impossible and a shovel recce was always inevitable. Now this is a true story we had a young lad straight from basic training Private Kevin Stroaker we aptly named him Willie, now he came up with a great idea while he was sorting the compo out and that was to use one of the empty ten man packs for a toilet which would save us squatting over a hole in the ground. All the ten man packs came with an outer sleeve for strength so Willie explained to us if we closed the empty box and replace the sleeve it was quite sturdy and you could sit on it, all you had to do was put a hole in the top and to do this he used a serrated knife like a saw, I think you have got the picture. The only problem was when you had done your business you would have to bury the whole box which entailed more digging due to its size. Willie was undeterred and decided he would dig the hole first then do his business in comfort then put the box in the hole to fill it in, we thought it was a good idea and thought nothing more of it. A few days later me and Seedy were cooking lunch when we heard this all mighty whoosh followed by a burst of flames and a scream which shook the trees. We knew Willie had gone for a shovel recce so we ran over to where the scream came from, when we found Willie he was sat on the ground holding a book of matches, he was covered with spots of shit it was in his hair all over his coveralls, in fact it was splattered everywhere we looked up to the trees to see bits of bog roll hanging from the branches and what was left of the compo box.

'What the fuck happened Willie?' said Seedy.

Willie got up of the ground the stench was putrid, we backed away at the same time.

'Well I used a box as usual,' he said, 'But I decided to bring a compo sugar tin full of petrol, my idea was to dig a smaller hole put the box in throw the petrol on and light it, then when it burns all the box away I just simply fill the hole in and I thought it would save me digging a huge hole for the box.'

The mistake Willie Stroaker made was throwing the petrol over the box with most of it going in the hole he had cut in the top, so when he threw the match in, the fumes exploded first, whoosh hehe. The SSM came running over and was none too pleased as we were supposed to be tactical at the time and Willie Stroaker got a right bollocking, It was funny because the sergeant major was about fifteen feet away from Willie as he was bollocking him, this was also one of the few times I wanted to hear the three words "Gas, Gas, Gas) which meant there was a gas attack and we would all put our gas masks on, the smell lingered for hours. One of the MT (motor troop) was detailed to take him to Reinselen so he could get a shower and cleaned up but he wouldn't let him ride in the front of the Bedford because of the stench and poor old Willie had to get in the back. He was very lucky he didn't come off worse than what he did but we had a good laugh about it later, good old Willie Stroaker and what a character he was.

When we got back to camp from exercise all the opened compo boxes would go into the main kitchen store to be used up, stewed steak was perfect for the larder cook who would make individual pies and pasties for the hotplate. I haven't mentioned breakfast much so will just sneak this in here before I carry on with the meat and potato pie. Lefty Wright came up with a neat little trick for the fried eggs on a morning he saved all the margarine tins and opened them at both ends then he placed them in the large frying pan on the burner, he then cracked an egg into each one allowing them to cook without spreading all over the pan once they were set he lifted the tins from the frying pan ready for the next batch they looked good all lined up on the serving trays and all the same size. The bacon grill was like a savoury luncheon meat and when it was cut thin and fried it was spot on, baked beans were in most packs, some had little sausages mixed with the beans, other packs had just sausages, these were the troops favourite. If you ever see an old veteran just ask him what he thought of compo sausage? Chances are it will be a big thumbs up. I have even seen compo sausages made into sausage rolls on exercise.

Right let's make meat and potato pie just like my mother used to make, I am on location in Lingdale north Yorkshire as I make this, my critics will be Bill and Sandra the owners of the barn cottage where we are staying this week, they have already tested my lasagne and I think they approved.

*****

Lean diced beef 1 ½ lb.

Half a cup of seasoned plain flour.

Four onions chopped.

Four carrots peeled and diced.

Baby potato's quartered or normal potato's peeled and diced 2lb

Water about a pint.

Salt and pepper.

Short pastry.

First of all, coat with the beef with the seasoned flour and seal well, sometimes it is better to do it in small batches, put in the slow cooker.

Fry the carrots and onions in the beef residue for a few minutes, then add the water and bring to the boil, once boiled leave for a couple of minutes then put in the slow cooker, I am going to forget about it now till we get back this afternoon. I have cooked the potato's and drained them for later.

Put the cooked meat in the pie dish as shown above and let it cool pile the potatoes on before covering with the nice thick pastry, egg wash and cook in the oven about 140 for 45 minutes till golden brown. Lovely grub with buttery mash and garden peas.

ALICE'S EASY RICH CAKE

Maybe not as easy as I thought because I made a right bollocks of the first batch I made, however later on in the day I realised what I done wrong and should have seen it in the first place, firstly the fruit sunk to the bottom and secondly Mandy pointed out to me that it was more sponge like than fruit cake I had used caster sugar and more eggs in the mix which made the mix thinner allowing the fruit to sink I have now rectified the recipe as you will find out below

Remember I told you about the ginger pudding which could be sliced up and used as cake, there was another pudding that I haven't mentioned yet and that is Mixed fruit pudding very similar in texture to a Christmas pudding but sliced up cold with a mug of coffee it was delicious. The real compo cake though was Rich cake when the tin was opened at both ends you pushed the cake out and I remember it was lined with greaseproof, like lots of other compo items this cake was cooked in the tin, rich cake would normally be cut up and served at lunch time, it was one of the nicest fruit cakes I have ever tasted. If we ever managed to scrounge some jelly crystals from the cookhouse before we deployed, we could make trifles using the rich cake and compo fruit, top it with custard and if we caught the local farmer in a good mood, we would bribe him with jams and marmalade for some fresh cream. Another thing I haven't mentioned yet is the chocolate bars and boiled sweets, there were five bars in the tin plus assorted boiled sweets. All the compo packs had a little white book of matches for lighting the hexamine blocks for the portable cookers and of course we used them to light the number one burner. I haven't mentioned the twenty four hour pack yet mainly because it was very rare we got them issued, these packs were mainly for infantry and self-sufficient soldier's however I do remember the matches they contained they were waterproof, they were bulbous things and when you struck them they burned slowly you could stick them in bowls of water and they would still burn. I have recently looked them up on amazon and they are called storm-proof matches and they are exactly the same costing £7.99 for 25.

When I first joined the army, the chocolate in compo was Tiffin if any of you can remember that, then it changed to plain dairy milk chocolate and apparently before my time there was Bournville. Chocolate was always in demand especially the married soldiers who would stash it in their bags to take home for the kids. I chose this recipe for my top 50 because of its simplicity in making, I used it regularly when I worked in the old folks home as it is versatile, you can use your electric whisk for the creaming and eggs, it isn't a MACs recipe it is one that I picked up over the years as a civilian.

Anything was possible in the field all it took was a bit of forethought and cheek with the farmers.

Rich fruit cake for 12 pieces.

*****

Softened butter 6oz

Dark brown sugar 6oz

Marmalade 3 tablespoons

Sr flour 8oz

Eggs beaten 3

Mixed dried fruit's 14oz

Mixed spice one teaspoon

Sliced almonds 1oz

Glace cherries 1oz cut in half

140

Quiche Separabit

*****

Cream the butter and sugar together for two minutes, it is easier if you have a mixer.

Add the marmalade and whisk for another minute.

Add the eggs carefully a little at a time, if the mixture does curdle then add some of the flour.

This is where I changed the method slightly and rather than putting all the flour, fruit, almonds and spice into the creamed mix I put them in another bowl as shown above, I used a pan. Then thoroughly mix all the fruit in with the flour ensuring everything is coated. Then scrape the creamed mixture onto the dried fruit and flour and mix well. This ensures that the fruit will stay put and not sink.

Pour into a loaf tin, I greased and lined mine plus I had enough mix left to make nine tester buns for the kids.

Cook in the oven at 140, I cooked this one in the Halogen oven for about 95 minutes, after 30 minutes I turned it down to 120, just keep your eye on it. This is another of those tried and tested recipes that I have used for years, I cannot remember where I got it from but it does work. Just don't forget to mix the fruit with the flour first. Test with a skewer if it comes out clean its cooked, then leave on a wire rack to cool. This second one turned out okay and I was pleased with the finished product, but I don't think the master chef would have been pleased with my first attempt.

CHICKEN MARYLAND

Southern fried chicken or chicken Maryland as we called it, this is a very simple dish but it was quite time consuming especially doing it for 50 people in the main camp kitchen where we had all the facilities. It was mainly the garnish for it that took the time and the master chef would want it doing correctly or we would be in the shit. Chicken breast in breadcrumbs with corn fritters, fried bananas in breadcrumbs and bacon rolls. It looks great and very professional as you can see above. Every time the menu board was put up in the kitchen there would be sighs all round, it seemed like it was chicken Maryland all the time it was a balls ache. Now you don't have to bother with the garnish unless perhaps you are impressing your friends, so if you just want to do the chicken for a salad or whatever then go ahead. I have done it over the years while working in the old people's home and have put it into my top fifty because we could do it with the compo plus, I love chicken in breadcrumbs anyway. I have tried my hardest to find a coating like KFC do, crushed cornflakes, rice crispie's, wholemeal breadcrumbs, Ryvita, cheese crackers, spices and herbs but I cannot get that taste.

So how did we do it in the field you may ask? My army colleagues from my era will remember that in the compo, I think it was the F pack there used to be chicken in brown sauce, no! not HP sauce but a thick unappetising gravy, I think it was one of the least popular meals in all the compo rations which was eventually removed from the packs. On exercise it was mainly good for chicken pies, but it was often the least popular choice on the menu.

When we opened the tins, the chicken was still in breast strips about 2 inches long so it was quite chunky. Once when we were on a German farm, we decided to wash the gravy off the chicken in cold water. After bartering with the old farmer with our jam, cheese we managed to get some onions, mushrooms, tomatoes ect, we would cook the compo rice and make a savoury chicken risotto with some of the ingredients the farmer had given to us, finally bit of salt and pepper and hey presto that ghastly chicken in brown sauce was transformed into something more presentable and edible as basic as it may sound. It was Seedy Simpson who came up with the idea of egg and bread crumbing the chicken one night as we sat around a burner having a beer, once we had washed it off we rolled it in seasoned plain flour, then egg washed it, and finally into the bread crumbs that we had sieved through a colander and it worked a treat. We then fried the two-inch strips in the compo margarine, it was surprising how much chicken there was when we opened about forty tins, it was a fantastic transformation in both texture and taste.

Let's prepare chicken Maryland.

*****

Two chicken breasts.

Two eggs whisked.

Seasoned plain flour.

Breadcrumbs mixed with black pepper, paprika, garlic powder.

Oil for frying.

One banana peeled cut into quarters.

Sweet corn.

Small amount of pancake batter.

Two rashes of bacon rolled.

Salt and pepper.

Sprig of fresh parsley.

143

*****

Cut the chicken breasts so you have four pieces, season with salt and pepper then dip in the seasoned flour, dip in the egg wash then finally in the breadcrumb mix.

Do the same with the bananas

Make a very small amount of thick pancake batter, put in some sweet corn and mix.

Cook the bacon and keep warm

(These garnishes are totally optional so if you just want to do the chicken it is your choice)

Fry the chicken on both sides till cooked and golden brown then put in the oven to keep hot.

Drop the corn mixture into the hot frying pan using clean oil and a tablespoon they need to be about 50p coin size. Fry the banana next till golden brown, keep the garnish warm.

Put the chicken on a platter then put the garnish round as shown, I think it looks quite impressive and so did my good neighbours who had the pleasure of eating it.

XMAS MINCE PIES

I used to watch my mother making these little pies the traditional way when I was a kid that lovely Christmassy smell lingers in my mind to this day. In the early 70s we used to make hundreds and hundreds of them for the regiment at Christmas mainly for the squadron kids party's there was no readymade buy them from the shops in those days. Me and Seedy could probably make about 400 in one day they were quite easy to do, they were just tedious and time consuming, but Seedy was always looking for a short cut. We used to get big blocks of puff pastry and Seedy told the master chef he had a good idea to make a different type mince pie, I don't know how he did it but he convinced the chef to let him make 100. It wasn't Seedy's invention he told me he had seen it somewhere and it stuck in his mind, at the time I wasn't convinced. It was so simple we just rolled the puff pastry out as thin as possible almost like filo pastry, then we spread the pastry with the mincemeat and rolled it up like a swiss roll. All we had to do now was cut them up into thin slices and lay them on the baking trays, egg wash them and in the oven. They looked similar to Danish pastries that you get with continental breakfasts or small Chelsie buns, apart from doing these we had the Christmas cakes on the go and we would also have to make little fruit jelly's and sandwiches for the kids. When I was looking for my recipe stories for this book, I searched the internet to see if I

145

could find these puff pastry things that Seedy had us making that day and apparently, they are called mincemeat pinwheels, so Seedy had seen them somewhere at the time. Seedy had this knack of convincing people as he did with the master chef that day I will never forget when he told us this story and it sounded outrageous at the time. He told us he had got a sexually transmitted disease from some bird in the Django bar, so to make it look like he was the innocent party when he got home he told his wife that he had an itch on his cock and had been to see the doc in medical centre where he was diagnosed with a dose of the clap. Seedy then went home and he turned the tables on her and called her a slut accusing her of sleeping around and that he had caught it off her. Upset and crying she too went to the medical centre to get tested and the doctor told her she had got the clap as well. When she got home and told Seedy, the poor lass apologised, but swore she hadn't been with anyone, Seedy told her not to worry and that she had probably caught it of a toilet seat in the community centre. Now I never met Seedy's wife he never brought her to any of the cook's parties and the reason for this I believe was so he could sow his wild oats whenever the opportunity came up, or in Seedy's case when something else came up hehe. After he told us this story, I thought his wife must be a very gullible or a stupid woman, either that or she loved him very much. I never saw Seedy again and when I transferred to the regiment years later, I got talking to one of the cooks who had known him and he told me he had shared a room with him in Osnabruck, he told me he was always sneaking women into the accommodation block late at night and he couldn't get to sleep because of Seedy's sexual activities, I asked why was he living in the barracks? And was told that his wife had left him years ago. She had most likely seen Seedy for what he really was.

*****

Sweet paste recipe from my apple pie

Mince meat

Beaten egg to glaze icing sugar for dusting

Pre heat the oven to 150 or 140 fan ovens

Divide the sweet paste into eight, I am doing the larger ones here, out of this mix you will get about a dozen in a tart tin.

Grease the tin and roll out the pastry, using a cutter line the tart moulds.

Fill the tart with the mincemeat, then cutting the tops slightly smaller put them on top as shown, egg wash and if you feel a bit cheffy put some leaves on, that's it simple.

I cooked them for 30 minutes at 140.

146

SWEET AND SOUR CHICKEN WITH RICE

Once when I was on exercise I was once given a challenge by a certain Quartermaster and that was to produce a Chinese meal out of compo. We were on Reinselen camp at the time Reinselen was the camp the troops would use on exercise for showers and toilets and on a weekend it was very busy, the regiment would park their vehicles up on the outskirts of the camp in their respective squadrons, then they would all pile into Reinselen for their shit, shower and shaves. Also, on the same evening they would have the famous squadron smokers which would be a bonfire, barbeque and loads of beer and I loved them.

'I want you to make me a Chinese meal out of compo Alice,' said the Quartermaster.

'That's a bit of an ask sir,' I said.

'Well if anybody can do it you can,' he said.

I looked at the ten-man compo packs then back at the QM.

'I will give it a go sir,' I said.

'I am looking forward to it,' he replied.

I sat down and stared at the boxes, I was only feeding the QM and his staff so that was one consolation, I already had flour and eggs so I went on the cadge around Reinselen camps field kitchens for some extras. I remember I came back with a couple of onions, cornflour, a tin of bean sprouts, some curry powder, vinegar, ketchup.

My goal was to impress the QM so I looked at what I had, I had an easy start with the tinned curried chicken, there was Patna rice in the compo that needed to be cooked so I could do egg fried rice with that, I made my trusty pancakes and with the bean sprouts and onion and a sprinkle of curry powder I made the spring rolls, I made some fresh flat breads, then I thought about sweet and sour chicken. I chopped a few tins of the compo fruit salad up, sliced some onions, put it all in a pan with vinegar, tomato ketchup and sugar once it boiled, I thickened it with cornflour. I remembered Seedy Simpsons egg and bread crumbed chicken, so I washed the brown sauce off and floured it, but rather than egg and breadcrumbs I made a batter and fried it. I made about half a dozen side dishes for the curry and laid everything out on the table, needless to say the QM and his staff ate everything on the table. For them it was a special treat and I have to say I was very pleased with what I had produced from those compo packs with the help of those few little extra ingredients that I had cadged. For this recipe below I will be egg and bread crumbing the chicken.

For two portions

*****

Two chicken breasts cut into scallops.

Fresh breadcrumbs

Cayenne pepper to taste.

Paprika to taste.

Salt and pepper

Egg wash

Seasoned flour

Patna rice, either cook your own or but the uncle bens microwaveable packets.

Sweet and sour sauce.

Vinegar 2oz.

Brown sugar 2oz.

Ketchup 6oz.

Small tin of pineapples and juice.

Spring onions chopped 2.

Or one-part vinegar, one-part sugar, three parts ketchup depending how much you want to make.

*****

Season the breadcrumbs with salt pepper, cayenne and paprika.

Egg and bread crumb the chicken pieces.

Cook half a cup of Patna rice or use the ready microwaveable stuff from the supermarket, pile it into the buttered ramakin dishes then cover with cling film ready for the microwave.

For the sauce combine all the ingredients in a pan except the spring onions, simmer for 5 minutes till it thickens slightly then add the spring onions.

Fry the chicken in oil till golden brown each side, meanwhile put the rice in the microwave for a couple of minutes.

The chicken shouldn't take long put it on some kitchen roll to drain the oil, turn the rice out onto a plate to get the timbale effect as above, lay the chicken out and just put a bit of sauce on the plate, garnish as you wish. It's simple and looks good, once you have all the ingredients ready you can cook this in ten minutes.

ALICE'S ALL IN CHRISTMAS PUDDING

The nearest thing to Christmas pudding in the compo was the mixed fruit pudding, as I said in my earlier recipes, we would use this as a cake sliced up, I liked it with a bit of compo cheese on, it's a Yorkshire thing. Seedy Simpson was a character he had so many cowboy recipes he made Clint Eastwood look like a cow hand, he once did a Christmas lunch for the sergeant's mess in barracks and couldn't be bothered to make Christmas pudding so he got some tins of mixed fruit pudding from the back store. He opened them all up and put them in the Hobart (kitchen mixer) with half a dozen eggs, a couple of handfuls of brown sugar, some mixed spice and cinnamon, almonds and half a bottle of sherry, he gave it a quick mix then he put it all into pudding basins, covered them and put them in the steamer for a couple of hours. When he turned them out onto platters, he put a few tots of brandy over the top with a sprig of holly and flambéd them, the waiter took them out to the table served with brandy sauce made of two pints of milk, sugar and thickened with cornflour and to finish it off he threw some brandy in. The compliments flooded back to the kitchen to Seedy's surprise as his compo adapted pudding gained him fame throughout the sergeant's mess. To add insult to injury the master chef was lunching that day with the senior ranks he came to the kitchen to compliment Seedy personally asking him for the recipe hehe, apparently it was the best homemade Christmas pudding he had ever tasted, it was a good job the master chef was half cut, Seedy's face went as white as a sheet, he was a star of the first order hehe.

In the main kitchen the CO would be there to stir the pudding before it went in the steamers, this was a bit of a tradition for our regiment and it happened every year. Another tradition a week or so before Christmas was the soldiers Christmas dinner where all the senior ranks and officers would serve the troops with their xmas lunch in the main dining room. Tables would be set up for them with cloths, crackers and few beers each. The sergeant majors would always warn them beforehand about their behaviour during the meal but it was to no avail, a lot of them would have a few drinks in the squadron bars before coming for their lunch, the louder ones were the ones that the RSM was watching. The Christmas spirit had set in and the soldiers for once had the upper hand, well at least they thought so, they would don their party hats and start on the free beer; soup would be served by suspicious senior ranks and nervous officers. The troops would eat their soup then when the main course was served the first sprout would fly across the dining room, this would be followed with a spoon of mashed potato, stuffing and carrots, empty cans the food fight had started, senior ranks and officers would be ducking and diving to avoid the food missiles. The RSM would normally step in and bring everything back under control with his authority, by then though it was too late and the dining room looked like Hiroshima. At the end of the meal they would start singing Christmas carols accompanied by the regimental band whose uniforms were splattered with what was once Christmas dinner, slowly they would file out to their respective squadron bars the RSM watching them with his mill board and pen poised as they left the dining room, the unsuspecting instigators would be in front of him the next day for a bollocking and their Christmas extra duties.

This recipe is for 6 to 8 people in true Seedy style and you don't even need kitchen scales, for the butter just cut a 250g block in half, you will need a one-pint basin or individual ones like mine, if this is too much half the ingredients accordingly.

*****

Mixed dried fruit 2 cups

Brown sugar 1 cup

Soft butter 1 cup or 4oz

SR Flour 1 cup

Breadcrumbs brown 1 cup

Assorted nuts 1 cup (optional)

Milk 1 cup

Eggs 1

Mixed spice one level teaspoon.

Cinnamon one level teaspoon.

Put the first six cups in the mixing bowl with the spices, if you are using the nuts put them in too, give it a quick mix then stir in the milk and egg and combine well, put the mixture into your pudding basins and cover with greased tinfoil ensure they are sealed around the edges. Either put in a steamer or like me in the slow cooker make sure the water is half way up the pudding bowl, check the water level during the cooking, top up with boiling water if needed. Cook for about 2 to 3 hours I just leave them for about 4 hours. Once cooked turn out onto a plate and serve with brandy or butterscotch sauce.

Butterscotch sauce

Brown sugar 2oz.

Butter 2oz.

Golden syrup 1oz.

Vanilla essence.

Double cream 2 ½ oz

Put the sugar, butter, golden syrup and vanilla in a pan and bring to the boil, turn the heat down as it starts to thicken, don't leave it, then had the double cream stir and pour over the puddings.

If you want to freeze them until Christmas wrap in cling film and tinfoil. You can prepare this early and cook it on Christmas day it is not as heavy as a normal pudding and tastes lovely. To be honest it is cheaper to go and buy one from the supermarket these days and less hassle but for me this brought back memories from my cookhouse days so it is up there with my favourite recipes, plus it brought a few smiles to my face while I was writing and mixing it. I think even Seedy Simpson would be proud of me for this recipe.

FRIKADELLEN

I am down to the last of the compo foods that I can remember now, some of my old friends will remember the compo beef burger which was a lunch choice, like bacon burgers there were five beef burgers in a tin. The bacon burgers we would take out of the tins split them into five, then tray them up and oven cook them for breakfast, like the compo sausage they were very popular at breakfast and not to be mixed up with bacon grill which we sliced up before frying similar to spam. I used to love a compo breakfast myself while on exercise it really did set you up for the day.

The beef burgers were the same we opened the tins and split them into five on a baking tray with loads of onions, the troops used to love them for lunch, sometimes we would pour gravy over them and braise them for the evening meal to give the blokes an extra choice and finally if it was all in stew we would just chop them up and throw them in the pot. Before I continue with my frikadellen recipe there is one last item of compo that I did mention briefly earlier in this book but haven't used it at all and that was the pilchards in tomato sauce, I think they were one of the least liked things in the compo packs. To use them we just opened them up and put them on a tray near the jams, margarine, chocolate, oatmeal blocks and sweets at lunch times and if the troops wanted them, they could eat as many as they wanted and good luck to them. When I first used compo in the early 70s, I have to admit I quite liked them probably because I was fond of sardines which we used to get at home when we were kids, my dad used to like them on toast. Anyway, we put the pilchards out for lunch one day on FTX (field training exercise) one of the young lads complained because the pilchard he had taken was full of little eggs.

'Have you never eaten caviar?' joked Seedy Simpson.

The young lad shook his head nervously.

'You don't know what you are missing!' laughed Seedy.

I could see the bulging pregnant pilchard in the lad's mess tin it looked disgusting. To be fair there was not a lot Seedy could have done as we were on exercise and it came out of a tin, it could have happened to anybody.

The lad scraped his mess tin into the bin as Seedy looked on smiling.

As for me I never ate them again ever.

Frikadellen is a German pan-fried meat pattie similar to a beef burger and in my top 50 favourites, I got this recipe off a German landlady years ago and was surprised to find out they were made with both beef and pork, She used to make a large batch every week and we could smell them from the bar area when she was cooking them in the kitchen. When she finally brought them through, they went like wild fire especially while they were still warm. I used to love them with plenty senf which was a mild German mustard, you can buy them in Lidl but they are not the same, try making your own you could probably use them for barbeques.

This is a tried and tested recipe they are simple to make and delicious give it a go.

For four frikadellen.

*****

Beef mince ½ 250 g

Pork mince ½ 250g

Two slices of bread diced crusts cut off.

Egg 1

Finely chopped onion cooked

Fresh chopped parsley

Paprika one teaspoon

Salt and pepper

154

Simply mix everything together, cover and fridge for 30 minutes then form into four to six flattened meatballs, fry in a pan steady till brown about 5 minutes each side then I popped them in the oven for 25 minutes at 140.

I just garnished with a bit of salad as above I like to eat them hot or cold, serve with senf or mustard.

I have looked everywhere in supermarkets for senf and had no luck, but you can get it on Amazon for five or six quid if you are willing to splash out so I am going to order a jar for myself.

EASY CHRISTMAS CAKE

My penultimate offering is this easy fruit cake for Christmas very easy to make and decorate. Christmas time with the 4/7ᵗʰ RDG was always my favourite time of year, the lavish buffets not only for the officers and sergeants' messes but all the squadrons as well, more commonly known as the silly season, I surprisingly have very many happy memories of those boozy Christmas functions with the elaborate spreads and expensive Christmas draws where the top prizes were normally a car or a holiday. As soon as I smell Christmas cake cooking it reminds me of home when I was a kid, my mother would mix the ingredients and put it on a low heat in the oven the night before, the next morning when we woke up the house would smell gorgeous, a sign for us that it was Christmas time. As I write this now, I can still smell that beautiful aroma of Christmas in my mind. A few years ago, when I was working, I would prepare the Christmas cakes ready for the oven then take them all home and bake them in my own oven very slowly so I could get that memorable smell in our house. It was the same in the army kitchen huge quantities would be made and cooked in the pastry ovens, the waft of Christmas cake you could smell all over the camp.

December was a busy time for us cooks and there would be buffets to do every other day plus there were the squadron kids' parties to cater for in the afternoons. The master chef would organise a buffet team to do all the functions and that was their sole job all month. It was a good idea as it took the strain off the rest of the cooks who could concentrate on the normal meals for the troops. There was no specific finishing time for the buffet team you would arrive in the morning about 8.30am and crack on with the buffet, maybe in the afternoon when everything was done we would knock off for a few hours then return later to transport the food to the respective squadron and set up, then we would hang about till service, but it wasn't boring and we were always supplied with copious amounts of free beer so by the time the buffet started we were more pissed than the squadron personnel, sometimes it would be two or three in the morning before we fell into bed knowing that in five hours we would have to do it all again.

Seedy Simpson would often be in charge of the fruit soaking for the Christmas cakes, large six-gallon oval pots would be filled with the mixed fruits, cherries, mixed peel, mixed spice, cinnamon and Seedy would pour the bottles of brandy over it allowing it to soak overnight. The next day Seedy would strain the fruit leaving the residue brandy in the bottom, me and Lefty Wright would start to weigh up the rest of the ingredients. Seedy had strained the booze into a jug and we would taste the fruity brandy on our break time, it was a punch with a difference hehe, it was potent stuff and blew your fucking brains out. Once Seedy started beating the butter and sugar in the mixer we were wobbling all over the place, there were eggs and flour everywhere as he accidently put the Hobart machine on too fast it was like one of them circus shows with the clowns Lefty was trying to mop up the mess, we were giggling and tittering like schoolgirls we finally got the fruit mixed in and we poured it into the large baking trays ready for the oven hoping and praying it would be okay or we would have to face the wrath of the master chef. Once it was in the oven it gave us chance to clean the pastry department which look like a bomb had hit it, there was more flour and mix on us than what was in the oven. Seedy had been asked by one of the Squadron Sergeant Majors if he would be Santa clause for the kids Christmas party in the squadron bar which he had avidly agreed to.

'There will be a few beers in it for you Simpson,' said the SSM.

That's all that Seedy wanted to hear.

'I will be there sir,' said Seedy.

Once we got the pastry department cleaned up and still fuelled up with the brandy punch from the Christmas cake fruit me and Seedy set off to the squadron bar, leaving Lefty with the Christmas cakes. After a few beers I was chatting away when the SSM tapped me on the shoulder and asked me if I had seen Seedy, I told him I hadn't seen him for a while, in fact he had been gone over an hour.

'You will have to do Santa Alice,' said the SSM, 'The kids are waiting.'

So, half cut I got the Santa gear on and went to give the kids their presents, this was the first time I had done Santa and I hated it I felt so uncomfortable, I was cursing Seedy under my breath as I was giving the excited kids their gifts. When I had almost finished, I saw Seedy return to the bar he had been gone for almost two hours now, when I got back to the bar, Seedy was just finishing explaining to the Sergeant Major.

'Thanks for doing that Alice,' he said, 'I just told the SSM I had to go home for something.'

'You never told me,' I said.

'Well her its complicated,' he said, 'I will tell you later.'

It was complicated alright just another excuse for Seedy to get his leg over.

Seedy was like a bloodhound and once he got a whiff that the local regiments were going on exercise or Northern Ireland, he would sniff the wives out, once he had found his prey, he would be in the married block like a rat up a drain pipe. He told me he had once been with a married woman and he left his cap badge in the husband's number two dress pocket in the wardrobe. Apparently when the husband finally returned from his deployment and put his uniform on, he would find half a dozen different cap badges in his pockets, don't know whether it was true but it made me laugh.

Right let's get on with the Christmas cake.

*****

1kg of mixed fruit any blend of raisins, sultanas, currents, mixed peel, glace cherries, dried apricots, dates whatever you have in stock.

150ml sherry, rum, brandy (I am using port) plus extra for feeding the cake and a couple of tots for me while I mix the cake.

Zest and juice of lemons 2

250g pack of unsalted butter.

250g brown sugar.

4 eggs.

Two teaspoons of vanilla extract.

Two level teaspoons of cinnamon.

Two level teaspoons of mixed spice.

158

200g plain flour

100 g of flaked almonds, walnuts.

Put the fruit, almonds, spices, lemon juice and zest in a bowl with your choice of alcohol cover and leave to soak overnight.

Heat the oven to 120, butter and double line a cake tin, make sure the parchment is 3cm over the top of the tin.

Beat the butter, sugar and vanilla till creamy then beat in the eggs one by one, tip in the flour, soaked fruit and any liquid from the bowl and stir in, scrape it all into the tin. With the back of the spoon make a slight dent in the centre of the cake, then bake for 1 hour 45 minutes. I used the halogen oven again.

After one hour I reduced the oven from 120 to 110, cover the top with some foil if you think it is browning too quick and bake for another 45minutes to an hour. Use a skewer to test, poke it to the bottom of the cake if it comes out clean it is cooked. Once cool turn out and store in a tin, every so often feed both it and yourself with alcohol.

After a few weeks roll some marzipan and cover the sides and the top of the cake and trim, I normally roll it out and put the cake on the marzipan upside down to get a more accurate trim, you should brush the top of the cake with warm apricot jam before putting the marzipan on, I didn't have any so I used marmalade, put back in the sealed container for a few days.

Roll out the icing same as the marzipan but roll it thinner to cover the top and the sides, you can just do a round for the top if you wish as your Christmas paper or ribbon will cover the sides. You can slightly wet the marzipan with a touch of water to help the icing stick once again leave for a few days.

If you haven't got a smoother like me use a white mug, decorate at will indulge yourself. Store it in a tin till Christmas and there you have it all ready for cutting I love it with a chunk of cheddar cheese.

TOURNEDOS ROSSINI

Before I do this final recipe there is one compo item I have failed to mention and it is probably the most important thing in the ration pack, without it the tank crews would not have been able to eat their food. It is the trusty compo can opener which most squaddies carried on their key rings, I still have a few thrown about the house somewhere to this very day. When I first saw one of these as a young lad, I honestly didn't have a clue what they were for till someone explained it to me. In a static field kitchen, we sometimes had the luxury of the rotary can opener, but most of the time we had to rely on these handy little tools. Looking on eBay recently I saw that they were selling from

 £2 to £10 each wow! There was one in every compo pack and I wish now I had saved them all I would have had thousands to sell.

I cooked Tournedos Rossini for the officer's mess on quite a few occasions and it remains to be one of my favourite steak recipes, plus this is a bit of a tribute to a chef who taught me a lot and was a very good friend of mine and it wasn't Seedy or Lefty. When I first met my future wife Mandy this is one of the first things, I cooked for her, well you have to impress a lady don't you? Now in my version I have altered the ingredients slightly and used mushrooms instead of truffle simply because

161

truffle is about £78 an ounce and in the place of Madeira sauce, I have done pepper sauce. I said there would be no Escoffier type recipes in this book and has it happened he had something to do with this recipe while working in the Savoy hotel back in the 19th century named after the composer Gioachino Rossini. This is comfort food at its best and doesn't come more luxurious than this. In the late 70s I worked in the officer's mess with a young chef about my age who really knew his stuff, he was very keen that everything was done correctly and his attention to detail was second to none. If he suspected that I was taking any short cuts or using cowboy methods he would pull me straight away and tell me the error of my ways. After speaking with the officer in charge of food (The food member) together they would create the menu, the dinner nights were an elaborate feast of food that I would never have thought of, he would always want four or five courses on the menu, I remember one time he put six courses on. At the time I was very 1970s with my cooking things like prawn cocktail, egg mayonnaise and melon balls were my repertoire hehe. This young chef showed me the menu he had composed of Blinis with caviar, Consommé, Tornados Rossini, souffle Saxon royal.

The painstaking process of taking the sinew and fat off 70 fillet steaks then tying them so they were all the same size as the round of bread that would become the base for the steak. The foie gras pate would all have to be the same shape for the top of the fillet and shaved expensive truffle would be the topping, served with a rich Madeira sauce. The blinis were made from scratch it was similar to a crumpet pancake texture and was served with cream and caviar. The clear soup consommé would be made on the morning and finally the souffle was a pain in the arse but it looked fantastic when it was finished it was topped with a crown of choux pastry which was piped on the outer side of a metal pudding basin then cooked in the oven, we needed ten of these crowns and with them being so delicate they broke easily, I must have made fifty and if one was slightly broken he would have me do it again, great lad knew his stuff and ended up a master chef.

Tornados Rossini

*****

Two fillet steaks trimmed.

Sliced mushrooms plus two for the top of the steak.

One finely chopped onion

Brandy-egg cup full

Brussels pate cut into rounds.

Two rounds of bread.

Butter.

162

Double cream.

Pepper corns or cracked black pepper.

Salt.

Oil for frying.

Peel and stalk the two-mushrooms put a bit of butter in the top and microwave for 30 seconds.

Fry the bread both sides till brown and keep warm.

Season the steak and fry two minutes each side longer if you want them well done, let them fry don't mess with them in the pan at the same time fry the pate till coloured once the steaks are done put on a tray lay the pate on top and then place the cooked peeled cup mushroom on the pate, put in the oven 160 to keep warm.

Put all the sliced mushrooms in the frying pan with the onions and brandy, with a little more butter and cook till soft, put the cream in a jug with the black pepper or crushed pepper corns stir, then add to the mushrooms, season with salt, this won't take long to thicken so keep stirring then transfer to a jug or gravy boat.

Put the bread on the serving plate, then the steak combination and just a dribbling of the sauce for effect, serve the rest separately.

There you have it my favourite recipe of the book, if you were to order this in a restaurant, you would have to pay £20 or £30 maybe more, I did both these for less than a tenner. Try it yourselves you won't be disappointed.

AFTERWORD

Although my characters went under different names in this book, I never saw Seedy or Lefty again, perhaps if they read this book, they may recognise themselves. And as for the hapless Gopper Price whom I never met; I often wonder if he got his wish. However, a few years ago I was looking through the ACC corps roll and noticed there was a Sergeant Price from around that era. Maybe he changed his ways, who knows, maybe Seedy was telling us the truth.

I hope you have enjoyed reading my cook book and I hope you try some of the recipes, Thank you very much **MC**

Printed in Poland
by Amazon Fulfillment
Poland Sp. z o.o., Wrocław

50426673R00098